D0789731

Waterfalls of Nova Scotia: A Guide

Waterfalls
of Nova Scotia
A GUIDE

BENOIT LALONDE

GOOSE LANE

Copyright © 2018 by Benoit Lalonde.

All rights reserved. No part of this work may be
reproduced or used in any form or by any means,
electronic or mechanical, including photocopying,
recording, or any retrieval system, without the prior
written permission of the publisher or a licence from
the Canadian Copyright Licensing Agency (Access
Copyright). To contact Access Copyright, visit
www.accesscopyright.ca or call 1-800-893-5777.

Edited by Charles Stuart.
Cover and interior photographs by Benoit Lalonde.
Maps by Todd Graphic, www.toddgraphic.ns.ca.
Cover and page design by Julie Scriver.

Printed in China
10 9 8 7 6 5 4 3 2 1

We acknowledge the generous support of the
Government of Canada, the Canada Council for
the Arts, and the Government of New Brunswick.

Goose Lane Editions
500 Beaverbrook Court, Suite 330
Fredericton, New Brunswick
CANADA E3B 5X4
www.gooselane.com

Library and Archives Canada Cataloguing
in Publication

Lalonde, Benoit, 1974-, author
    Waterfalls of Nova Scotia : a guide / Benoit Lalonde.

ISBN 978-1-77310-022-7 (softcover)

1. Waterfalls--Nova Scotia--Guidebooks.
2. Nova Scotia--Guidebooks. I. Title.

GB1430.N8L35 2018   551.48'409716
C2017-906126-7

Je dédie ce livre à Édith qui partage mes aventures depuis plus de vingt ans. Depuis ce temps, deux nouveaux explorateurs se sont joint à notre équipe. Édith, Ève, et Zacharie, je vous remercie de votre patience et enthousiasme lors de nos nombreuses expéditions!

27. Black Hole Brook Fall

Contents

87. Bothan Brook Fall

Preface

I moved to Nova Scotia from central Canada in 1999 and soon discovered that this province had a lot of hiking opportunities. After exhausting a couple of trail guides and scouring the Internet for information about hiking trails, I was looking to pursue a different experience in the outdoors. A few years previously, Allan Billard published his first guide to the waterfalls of Nova Scotia (Billard 1997). I bought the book at the same time as some good friends of mine. After visiting the first fall from the book together, we challenged ourselves to a waterfall race. It did not take me long to visit most of the falls in this book and win the challenge. That is how my addiction to waterfalls started. Afterwards I found more falls to pursue by searching online. A few people (Dino Nardini and Steve Meredith) were exploring waterfalls in Nova Scotia and publishing the information online. However, I soon exhausted all those sources of information too! That is when I discovered some old digitized maps of Nova Scotia. These maps did not catalogue the whole province or all of the individual waterfalls, but they enabled me to seek many lesser-known falls. One last source of information that I exhausted was geocaching. A person on geocaching.com who goes by the name of Pushkin explored many remote waterfalls throughout Nova Scotia, and the information he shared has been useful. For a few years, I described a lot of my explorations on www.trailpeak.com. This website is a wonderful user-input source of information for any self-propelled adventure in Canada, the United States, and Mexico. This book is the result of all of these different sources of information and the many hours searching for waterfalls in the four corners of this province. In between those old maps, satellite imagery, and topographical maps, I have been able to located a few hundred falls. As of late 2017, I have visited more than six hundred individual waterfalls in Nova Scotia, and my list of places left to explore holds as many. My best advice for people who are starting to get into the rewarding pastime of seeking waterfalls is to never turn back, because you never know, the waterfall might be just around the next bend!

Introduction

The waterfalls in this guide are divided into sections that conform to Nova Scotia's familiar scenic route system. Therefore, waterfalls around the Halifax Regional Municipality are divided into two different trails (Lighthouse Route and Marine Drive). The information for each waterfall in this guide is provided to enable the reader to assess and choose which fall(s) to explore. This information includes important planning aspects such as hiking distance, time, and elevation as well as a rating for the level of difficulty to reach a waterfall. Other information listed for each waterfall includes the trailhead and waterfall GPS coordinates and a description of the hike and the fall itself. Each entry in this guide includes a map and a photograph of the fall.

Nova Scotia is blessed with numerous waterfalls, and paring the list down to one hundred was extremely difficult. I spend a lot of time searching for waterfalls throughout the province, and my first attempt at developing a list had over two hundred. Foremost, the list was developed to try and maximize the geographical distribution to cover the whole province (see fig. 1). Areas such as the Cobequid Hills or the Highlands of Cape Breton could easily include one hundred entries in each. The degree of difficulty to reach each fall was also assessed in order to have an equal number of falls in each category. An effort to maximize the type of waterfalls and scenic locations was also assessed to reach a final list of one hundred waterfalls.

Lastly, there are some falls that have been described previously in guidebooks that just cannot be omitted from this guide because they are classic waterfalls to discover in Nova Scotia, such as Garden of Eden Fall, Wentworth Fall, Cuties Hollow, Annandale Fall, and Butcher Hill Fall. However, there are other classic waterfalls that are not in this book but are easy enough to discover using provincial or federal government websites (NS Tourism, Parks Canada). These easy-to-find falls include Drysdale Fall (Tatamagouche), Howe and Waddell Falls (Truro), Manager's Park Falls (Londonderry), Borden Brook Fall (Blomidon Provincial Park), Baxters Harbour Fall (Baxters Harbour), South Brook Falls (Factorydale), Morgan Fall (LaHave River), TR's Fall (Sandy Cove, Digby Neck), Park Falls (Sutherlands River), Arisaig Fall (Arisaig Provincial Park), Corney Brook Fall (Cape Breton Highlands National Park), Economy River Fall (Economy), Beulach Ban Fall (Cape Breton Highlands National Park), Black Beach Brook Fall (near Neils Harbour), Mary Ann Falls (Cape Breton Highlands National Park), Uisge Ban Fall (near Baddeck), and Glenora Fall (near Mabou). I apologize to readers in advance if I have omitted their favourite waterfall from this book.

36. Butcher Hill Fall

How to Use This Book

Information for each fall in this book includes the following:

Name of the waterfall. Anecdotal name(s) are used when they could be found, and names identified by the Canadian gazetteer were also used whenever possible. If there were not any known names, the name of the fall is the same as the body of water where the waterfall is located. Please note also that the falls are numbered from 1 to 100; these numbers correspond to those found on the maps.

Type. Waterfalls in this guide are described using various adjectives such as tiered, cascade, horsetail, fan, true drop, etc. Sometimes a single waterfall may have one or more adjectives to describe it.

- **Tiered:** Type of fall that has multiple, distinct levels that may or may not have the water change directions.

- **Cascade:** Type of fall that loses elevation in a series of small steps.

- **Slide:** Type of fall that never loses contact with the rock surface behind it and does not have small steps.

- **Fan:** Type of fall that begins in a very narrow slot and widens all the way down to form a pyramid shape.

- **True drop:** Type of fall that does not have any contact with the rock wall behind it. Sometimes there is enough room to walk behind the veil of water.

Height. The waterfall heights in this book are not perfect measurements. A precise measurement of the height of a waterfall would require surveying equipment. Furthermore, the exact location of the start and end of a waterfall can be ambiguous. The heights of waterfalls listed in this guide were obtained either using the 1:10 000 topographical maps or by measuring them myself. The heights should only be used as a general guideline.

Best season(s). This is a tricky but important section to describe. Most watersheds in Nova Scotia are quite small and therefore do not have the capacity to retain water in the driest months. However, even in the driest months, all these streams can refill quickly when a downpour occurs. My rule of thumb in the drier months (yes, they do exist in Nova Scotia!) is to hunt for a waterfall after a rainfall of 30 mm (1.25 in) or more. In the spring and autumn, most falls will have enough water to make the trip worthwhile anytime. Don't stop exploring in winter. The true drop falls are my favourite type to see in the winter as they develop into giant icicles. Also, true drop type falls will not be engulfed by snow to the extent that they remain indiscernible. Usually, the waterfall hunting season without snow can occur from April well into late December or even early January. I associate one or more best seasons for each fall based on my own experience.

Access: This category is used to describe the type of journey encountered on the way to the waterfall.

- **Trail:** These are falls that have either official or well-established un-official trails leading to them.

- **Roadside:** These are the falls that are located very close to the road.

- **Bushwhack:** I use this word throughout the book. Some waterfalls have no trails to reach them, necessitating movement through uncleared bush. Depending on the forest type, it might be easy or difficult to push through the vegetation (bushwhack) on the way to the waterfall.

- **River walking:** Some waterfalls are accessed by walking in or very close to the edge of a stream. For example, sometimes the cliffs surrounding the streams cannot be bypassed except by walking in the river itself.

- **Shore walking:** A few waterfalls can only be accessed by walking on the seashore (Russia Road Brook Fall, Black Hole Brook Fall). It is **imperative** that you consult a tide chart before setting off.

Source. Name of the brook, river, or lake associated with the waterfall. In a very few cases, the brooks were not named on the 1:10 000 or 1:50 000 topographical maps. In those cases, a nearby geographical feature was used to name the waterfall (e.g., Green Hill Fall).

Distance (one way). The hiking distances are estimated using the GPS track from the trailhead to the fall. The distance will vary depending on the navigational skills of the hiker and the route chosen to reach the fall. All distances are given in metric units and imperial measurements.

Difficulty. The degree of difficulty is related to the potential hazards encountered during the hike to a fall. The degrees are easy, moderate, difficult, and extreme.

- **Easy:** The waterfalls rated as easy are perfect for families with young children and/or can be suitable for a dog walk.

- **Moderate:** Waterfalls rated as moderate are falls that may not have paths to them or may have a moderate elevation gain/loss. Most people should be able to make it to these falls, but there might be some easy to moderate bushwhacking involved.

- **Difficult:** A difficult rating for a waterfall is something to seriously consider before planning your exploration. The fitness of the hiker and/or navigation skills will come into play for these hikes, and they should only be attempted after carefully evaluating the information in this book.

- **Extreme:** There are a few falls in this book that are rated as extreme. The extreme ratings should not be taken lightly as the terrain to get to these falls can be very dangerous. The remoteness of some of the falls might also be one of the reasons why they are designated as difficult or extreme. Such falls should be considered only by quite fit and able hikers.

Elevation. I have also included the total height of ascent as per my GPS track. Sometimes, even if a fall is not very tall, there might be a lot of ascent to tackle in the journey to the fall. Alternatively, a waterfall located in a deep ravine will seem to have a short ascent but can be very steep over a short section.

Hiking time. Some people describe me as a mountain goat because of my fondness for difficult terrain. The path I follow may be too steep for some people, and therefore the distance and/or time to each waterfall may be slightly underestimated. In general, the maximum distance a hiker can cover in one hour is about 3 km (1.9 mi) when not following a dedicated path, and sometimes much less if there is dense vegetation or lots of elevation gain/loss. Since these waterfalls are often in hard-to-reach locations, a buffer of time should be included in your plan to get back to your car during daylight hours.

Land ownership. Using open source software from the Nova Scotia government (https://novascotia.ca/parksandprotectedareas/plan/interactive-map/), the terrain of the trail and waterfall is qualified as private, Crown land, or protected (Nature Reserves, Wilderness Areas, National Parks). Although some of the waterfalls lie on private land, only waterfalls that did not have any private property signage or where their enjoyment would not be to the detriment of the landowners were included in this guide. A fellow explorer and waterfall enthusiast has explained the intricacies of waterfall access in Nova Scotia on his blog page (http://nswaterfalls.blogspot.ca/2013/07/a-shortish-note-on-waterfall-access.html).

Maps. Topographical maps of the province are available for free online. The Government of Canada provides free 1:50 000 topographical maps on a website called Geogratis (http://atlas.gc.ca/toporama/en/index.html) while the Nova Scotia provincial government provides free 1:10 000 topographical maps at GeoNOVA (https://gis8.nsgc.gov.ns.ca/DataLocatorASP/main.html).

Nearby waterfall(s). Since sometimes a long car trip from your home to the trailhead is necessary, it makes sense to visit more than one waterfall at a time. In general, the falls in this guide are listed in order of their proximity to each other. If some other waterfalls are located close by but are included in a different section of this book, they are listed under this heading.

Cellphone coverage. The cellphone coverage is based on the maps provided by the carriers. However, it is safe to assume that in most deep ravines there is no cell coverage as there are no direct lines of sight to cell towers. For safety considerations, the purchase of a GPS-based communication device such as a SPOT is your best option, as it should function even in deep ravines.

Fees and permits. The only waterfall in this book where a fee will be required is for Mill Fall as it lies in the Kejimkujik National Park. A daily fee is charged to all visitors to the park.

Finding the trailhead. The directions to the falls in this guide lead to an area located as close as possible to the falls but reachable by motor vehicle. Some of the roads might be used for logging operations or might be in disuse and therefore require higher clearance. In those cases, a longer walk will be necessary to reach the trailhead and fall. The distances were obtained using a car odometer or Google Maps so they are approximate at best.

Trailhead. These are the GPS coordinates of the trailhead. The trailhead might be the start of the trail or the general area to enter the wood. In some cases, the trailhead is located at the beginning of a dirt road since all vehicles have different height clearances and drivers have different levels of comfort driving these dirt roads. In a very few instances, I have also provided contact information for the trail/fall.

Waterfall. These are the global positioning system (GPS) coordinates in degrees, minutes, and seconds of the waterfall itself. Depending on the canopy coverage and height of the ravines surrounding it, the location might be slightly incorrect.

The hike. This section is split into two parts. The first is a general description of the area around the fall, the fall itself, historical/geographical remarks, and any personal observations that I may wish to share. The second describes the actual directions to the fall.

Bonus fall(s) or **Bonus feature:** This section describes other nearby attractions. The bonus material does not include as much information as the main waterfalls of this guide, but a quick Internet search should reveal more details.

Mapping. The easiest way to ensure a visit to each waterfall is to record the latitude and longitude in a GPS device. All latitude and longitude coordinates used in this guide were obtained using the NAD83 datum and are given as degrees, minutes, and seconds. Online converters can transform those latitudes and longitudes into other formats such as universal transverse Mercator (UTM) or into decimal degrees. All the maps featured in this guide have a north heading grid at the top of the figure.

Photographs. One photograph for each fall is included in this guide. The difficulty was to find an image that gives a sense of the splendour waiting to be discovered. Of course, pictures of waterfalls rarely render justice to these ethereal beauties.

Safety and Other Considerations

There are numerous safety considerations to consider before setting off on these journeys. The following short list of these considerations should not be considered exhaustive.

- For some of the waterfalls in this guide, a good knowledge of reading maps and using a compass will be necessary. Search and rescue groups such as Halifax Search and Rescue (https://halifaxsar.ca/map-compass-course), hiking groups such as Hike Nova Scotia (https://www.hikeno-vascotia.ca/ourses--workshops--navigation/), and outdoor retailers such as Mountain Equipment Co-op usually teach these kinds of courses. Of course, do not forget to bring a map and compass with you in the woods as electronic devices are subject to failure due to various reasons (dead battery, immersion, smashing, sporadic or non-existent cell or GPS signals, etc.).

- There are occasions where people get lost in the forest but can reach out by cellphone or satellite phone to 911. The search for lost persons in the forest will involve one of the twenty-four search-and-rescue groups located throughout Nova Scotia (https://novascotia.ca/dma/emo/ground_search_rescue/). These groups, in collaboration with the various police forces, specialize in searching for lost or injured persons. It is my hope that you will not need this resource.

- Before setting off on the longer hikes, plan a turnaround time. This is a predetermined time for you to turn around and get back to the vehicle even if you have not yet reached the waterfall. This is especially important for remote explorations to ensure that you exit the woods before dark.

- An itinerary should be left with someone who can raise alarms in case of a delayed return time. The itinerary should include details such as location, GPS track if available, time to return, and vehicle information.

- There are very active hunting seasons in Nova Scotia, so be prepared to wear bright orange gear during those seasons. There are different open seasons depending on location, species hunted, and type of weapon used. Schedules can be found on the Nova Scotia Government–Natural Resources website (https://novascotia.ca/natr/hunt/). That being said, the majority of the hunting season occurs during the fall months. A further advantage of wearing orange gear is that it is easier to spot if you become lost. A good rule of thumb I use during hunting season is not to explore for waterfalls when a vehicle is already parked near the trailhead.

• There is a lot more gear that should be brought when attempting long explorations in remote areas. A gear kit may include such items as a compass and map, GPS, cellular phone, whistle, fire-making kit (flint), first-aid kit, food, water purification device, space blanket, sun protection, small axe and/or knife, and a fishing kit. Extra clothing, a sleeping bag, stove and fuel, and a tarp to use as an emergency shelter could prove very useful on the longer or remote explorations. There are numerous websites to help you figure out exactly what you should bring. Websites with a lot of local knowledge can be found at http://avoidingchores.com, www.sarnovascotia.com, and https://www.hikenovascotia.ca/resources-hiking-safety. It is always a good idea to bring a light source. For example, a small LED headlamp weighs practically nothing but may help you get out of the woods past sunset if necessary. Depending on the season and area, a bottle of bug spray can prove to be extremely useful. Often, the area at the base of a waterfall is a perfect place for insects to emerge, and the lack of wind in the deep ravines enables the insects to remain around you.

• There are a few waterfalls described in this book that are located on the Bay of Fundy. A careful examination of a tide chart is extremely important before setting off on the hike. The Government of Canada provides seven-day predictions at the following website: http://www.tides.gc.ca/eng. Tide charts can also be purchased at marine/yachting supply stores. Newer GPS units may also have built-in tide charts.

• Weather in Nova Scotia tends to change quickly. A quick look at the hourly forecast on the day you are exploring will help you plan for changes of the upcoming weather.

• We are lucky to live in a province largely devoid of large predators. However, encounters with bears, coyotes, moose, or even angry porcupines may occur. Depending on the animal and circumstance, different behaviours should be undertaken. Again, there are websites that can help in this endeavour. In the last decade, I have come face to face with all of the animals listed above while looking for waterfalls. Luckily, all these encounters resulted in a frightened human and animal turning around and heading in opposite directions. However, in the last few years, a fellow waterfall explorer has had a very frightening episode with a charging moose in the Cobequid Hills, so please be alert on the trail.

• Unfortunately, there is some wildlife for which you have to be especially vigilant in Nova Scotia. One of the most disturbing trends is the prevalence of ticks that carry Lyme disease in more and more areas of the province. The Nova Scotia government has a lot of information on the following website: https://novascotia.ca/ticksafety/. The black-legged ticks are very small and therefore hard to detect. For example, when not engorged, ten black-legged ticks can fit across the face of a dime. A black-legged tick can transmit Lyme disease if attached and buried for 24-36 hours. Therefore it is important that you check yourself after hiking to determine whether you have any ticks attached to your body. A bull's-eye type rash can be indicative of a tick bite, but also be aware that the following symptoms (with or without the rash) can appear following a bite: fever, fatigue, muscle aches, headache, and joint pain. If caught early, a short course of antibiotic can be successful in treating this disease. If you have any doubt about exposure to ticks, please visit your family doctor.

• Another danger that you should be aware of is the presence of giant hogweed. A detailed fact sheet on this introduced species can be found here: https://novascotia.ca/natr/wildlife/biodiversity/pdf/hogweedfacts.pdf. The sap from this up to 5 m (16 ft) high plant can be very dangerous as it causes burns to the skin that are activated by exposure to ultraviolet radiation (sunshine). This plant has been found near Kentville, Sheffield Mills, Truro, Baddeck, Dartmouth, Wolfville, Grand Pré, and Halifax, and its range is likely expanding. If you suspect that some sap has transferred to your skin, you should wash the affected area with soap and water immediately and cover the area so it doesn't receive any sunlight. The sap from this plant can also cling to our clothes and boots and can cause an exposure days or weeks afterwards if not cleaned.

• Poison ivy can also be present in areas at the base of some falls. For example, the scree slope located east of the main fall of the East Branch Moose River gorge has a large patch of it. The Nova Scotia Museum has a page of information here: https://novascotia.ca/museum/poison/?section=species&id=58. You should familiarize yourself with the appearance of this plant before exploring. A good, basic rule of thumb is to stay away from three-parted (sometimes shiny) leaves. Any suspected contact area should be immediately and carefully rinsed with warm, soapy water. The oil from this plant can cling to your clothes or boots and may affect you days and weeks after exposure. Poison ivy in Nova Scotia is dominant in gypsum-rich areas but can be found along any watercourse or shoreline and in open forest.

• Most of the areas around waterfalls or in the ravines leading to them have very slippery and loose rocks. Some areas, such as near Martha Brook Fall, are full of holes that are nicely hidden by a deep moss cover. There is always some probability that you might twist an ankle or worse in those locations. Therefore, exploring with another person is always a great idea.

• The directions to the falls include active and inactive logging roads as well as old bridges over streams and rivers. A great idea is to always assess bridges before driving over them and to drive as slowly as possible on the logging roads. Furthermore, inactive logging roads can be very uneven and have lots of protruding rocks, vegetation, and missing or damaged culverts. Assess these hazards before proceeding.

• Most of the waterfalls in this guide are located on crown land and pose no issues for access. Some of the other falls are surrounded by private properties. Sometimes, you may need to ask permission to access these falls if a private property sign is posted. I have noted such instances in the text. Some falls have official signed trails to get to them (Indian Falls on the LaHave River), while others have well-worn but unofficial paths.

• A lot of waterfall sites have deep pools at their base that are perfectly suitable for swimming. Bringing a towel and swimsuit is strongly recommended. However, one has to be careful about swimming under the spray of the fall itself, which can be very powerful. Also be aware that floating objects may fall at any moment from the height of the fall.

• My last consideration is the least scientific one: Trust your instinct! If the slope looks too dangerous, the bridges too rickety, the journey too arduous, always trust your instinct and turn around before you get yourself into trouble.

Nova Scotia Waterfall Locations

Lighthouse Route
1. Beaverdam Brook Fall
2. Webber Lake Fall
3. Pockwock River Fall
4. East River Falls
5. Skerry Fall
6. Indian Falls
7. Apron Falls
8. Firebrook Fall
9. Mill Fall
10. Broad River Falls
11. Big Fall

Evangeline Trail
12. Meteghan River Falls
13. Weymouth Falls
14. Walsh Brook Fall
15. Digby Gut Fall
16. Moose River Fall
17. Tupperville Brook Falls
18. St. Croix Fall
19. Eel Weir Brook Falls
20. Delanceys Brook Falls
21. Black River Falls
22. Crystal Fall
23. Shingle Mill Fall
24. Russia Road Brook Fall
25. Church Vault Brook Falls
26. Coby Irving Brook Fall
27. Black Hole Brook Fall
28. Moores Brook Fall
29. Little River Fall
30. Duncanson Brook Fall
31. Fall Brook Fall (Ettinger Fall)

Glooscap Trail
32. Dawson Brook Fall
33. Little Meander River Fall
34. Green Hill Falls
35. Christie Brook Falls
    (Greenfield Falls)
36. Butcher Hill Fall
37. Falling Brook Fall
38. Chiganois River Falls
39. Rockland Brook Falls
40. Spencer Brook Fall
41. Gamble Brook Falls
42. East River (Five Islands) Fall
43. North River (Five Islands) Fall
44. Garden of Eden Fall

45. McCarthy Gulch Falls
46. McCallum Gulch Falls
47. East Branch Moose River Fall
48. West Branch Moose River Fall
49. McAlese Brook Falls
50. Ripley's Fall
51. Wards Fall
52. Horse Pasture Brook Falls
53. Wentworth Fall
54. Annandale Fall
55. Arrowhead Fall

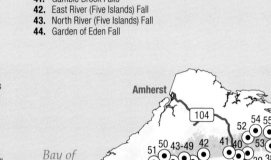

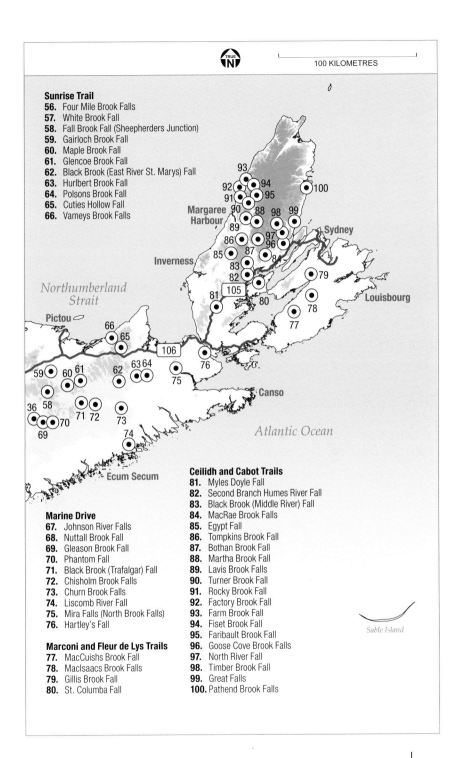

100 KILOMETRES

Sunrise Trail
56. Four Mile Brook Falls
57. White Brook Fall
58. Fall Brook Fall (Sheepherders Junction)
59. Gairloch Brook Fall
60. Maple Brook Fall
61. Glencoe Brook Fall
62. Black Brook (East River St. Marys) Fall
63. Hurlbert Brook Fall
64. Polsons Brook Fall
65. Cuties Hollow Fall
66. Vameys Brook Falls

Northumberland Strait

Pictou

Margaree Harbour

Inverness

Sydney

Louisbourg

Canso

Atlantic Ocean

Ecum Secum

Sable Island

Marine Drive
67. Johnson River Falls
68. Nuttall Brook Fall
69. Gleason Brook Fall
70. Phantom Fall
71. Black Brook (Trafalgar) Fall
72. Chisholm Brook Falls
73. Churn Brook Falls
74. Liscomb River Fall
75. Mira Falls (North Brook Falls)
76. Hartley's Fall

Marconi and Fleur de Lys Trails
77. MacCuishs Brook Fall
78. MacIsaacs Brook Falls
79. Gillis Brook Fall
80. St. Columba Fall

Ceilidh and Cabot Trails
81. Myles Doyle Fall
82. Second Branch Humes River Fall
83. Black Brook (Middle River) Fall
84. MacRae Brook Falls
85. Egypt Fall
86. Tompkins Brook Fall
87. Bothan Brook Fall
88. Martha Brook Fall
89. Lavis Brook Falls
90. Turner Brook Fall
91. Rocky Brook Fall
92. Factory Brook Fall
93. Farm Brook Fall
94. Fiset Brook Fall
95. Faribault Brook Fall
96. Goose Cove Brook Falls
97. North River Fall
98. Timber Brook Fall
99. Great Falls
100. Pathend Brook Falls

22. Crystal Fall

The **Waterfalls at a Glance** table (opposite) provides an overview of all waterfalls in this guide, their key features, as well as information re difficulty and cellphone coverage.

Type: T = Tiered   C = Cascade   S = Slide   F = Fan   D = Drop

Height: The height of the fall stated in metres (feet)

Season: The recommended season(s) for visiting the fall(s):
Spring = SP   Summer = S   Fall = F   Winter = W   Year-round = YR

Access: T = Trail   R = Roadside   B = Bushwhack required
RW = River Walking required   SW = Shore Walking required

Distance: Distance is provided as **one way**, in kilometres (miles) or metres/yards

Difficulty: E = Easy   M = Moderate   D = Difficult   X = Extreme

Elevation: The height of the fall(s) in metres/yards

Cell: The availability of cellphone coverage: Yes = Y   No = N

Waterfalls at a Glance

Waterfall	Type	Height m (ft)	Season	Access	Distance (one way)	Diff.	Elev.	Cell
LIGHTHOUSE ROUTE								
1. Beaverdam Brook Fall	T	5 (15)	SP, F	T	1.5 km (0.9 mi)	E	<20	Y
2. Webber Lake Fall	T	6 (20)	SP, F	T	150 m/yd	E	<20	Y
3. Pockwock River Fall	C	8 (25)	YR	T	1 km (0.6 mi)	E	40	Y
4. East River Falls	C	5 (15)	SP, S, F	R	200 m/yd	E	20	Y
5. Skerry Fall	C	5 (15)	SP, S, F	T	2.5 km (1.6 mi)	M	70	Y
6. Indian Falls	S	14 (45)	SP, F	T	200 m/yd	E	<20	Y
7. Apron Falls	S	8 (25)	SP, F	T	1 km (0.6 mi)	E	30	Y
8. Firebrook Fall	T	11 (35)	SP, F	R	200 m/yd	E	<20	Y
9. Mill Fall	S, D	8 (25)	SP, F	T	200 m/yd	E	<20	Y
10. Broad River Falls	C	5 (15)	SP	T, B	4.5 km (2.8 mi)	M	40	N
11. Big Fall	C	6 (20)	SP	B	1 km (0.6 mi)	M	<20	N
EVANGELINE TRAIL								
12. Meteghan River Falls	C	2 (6)	SP, F	R	10 m/yd	E	<5	Y
13. Weymouth Falls	T	15 (50)	SP	B	250 m/yd	E	30	Y
14. Walsh Brook Fall	T	8 (25)	SP, F	B	250 m/yd	M	30	Y
15. Digby Gut Fall	D, C, S	8 (25)	SP	RW, SW, B	3.5 km (2.2 mi)	M	150	N
16. Moose River Fall	T	6 (20)	SP	T	100 m/yd	E	<20	Y
17. Tupperville Brook Falls	C, T	15 (50)	SP	T	1.25 km (0.8 mi)	E	140	Y
18. St. Croix Fall	D	14 (45)	SP, F, W	T	150 m/yd	E-M	40	N
19. Eel Weir Brook Falls	D, T	12 (40)	SP	RW	1.1 km (0.7 mi)	M	85	N

Waterfall	Type	Height	Season	Access	Distance (one way)	Diff.	Elev.	Cell
20. Delanceys Brook Falls	T, C	2, 5, 5 (6, 15, 15)	SP, F	B, RW	500 m/yd	E	20	N
21. Black River Falls	T, C	5, 3, 6 (15, 10, 20)	SP	B, RW	1 km (0.6 mi)	E-M	40	N
22. Crystal Fall	D	8 (25)	SP, F	T	2 km (1.25 mi)	E	160	Y
23. Shingle Mill Fall	T	6 (20)	SP, S, F	T	1 km (0.6 mi)	E	40	Y
24. Russia Road Brook Fall	D	9 (30)	SP	SW	800 m/yd	E	<20	N
25. Church Vault Brook Falls	D, C, T	6 (20)	SP, F	RW	500 m/yd	E	30	Y
26. Coby Irving Brook Fall	D	12 (40)	SP, F, W	T	250 m/yd	E	<20	Y
27. Black Hole Brook Fall	D	12 (40)	SP, F, W	T, SW	1 km (0.6 mi)	M	100	Y
28. Moores Brook Fall	F	15 (50)	SP	RW	400 m/yd	M	<20	Y
29. Little River Fall	D, C	8 (25)	SP, F	T, B	1.75 km (1.1 mi)	M	140	Y
30. Duncanson Brook Fall	D, C, S, T	11 (35)	SP	T	1.5 km (0.9 mi)	E	120	Y
31. Fall Brook Fall (Ettinger Fall)	D	8 (25)	SP, F	R	1.25 km (0.8 mi)	E	40	Y
GLOOSCAP TRAIL								
32. Dawson Brook Fall	F	8 (25)	SP, S, F	T	700 m/yd	E	30	Y
33. Little Meander River Fall	D	6 (20)	SP	RW	1.25 km (0.8 mi)	E-M	100	Y
34. Green Hill Falls	F	14 (45)	SP	B, RW	1.2 km (0.75 mi)	M	80	Y
35. Christie Brook Falls (Greenfield Falls)	D	6, 6, 3 (20, 20, 10)	Year-round	T, B, RW	1.5 km (0.9 mi)	E-M	80	Y
36. Butcher Hill Fall	D, T	13.5 (44)	SP, F	T	200 m/yd	E	<20	Y
37. Falling Brook Fall	T	15 (50)	SP	T, B	3 km (1.9 mi)	M	150	Y
38. Chiganois River Falls	D, T, C	15, 9, 8, 6, 5 (50, 30, 25, 20, 15)	Year-round	B, RW	3 km (1.9 mi)	M	860	Y

Waterfall	Type	Height	Season	Access	Distance (one way)	Diff.	Elev.	Cell
39. Rockland Brook Falls	D, F	6, 9, 9 (20, 30, 30)	SP, F	RW	1.25 km (0.8 mi)	M	70	Y
40. Spencer Brook Fall	D	6 (20)	SP	T	800 m/yd	E	50	Y
41. Gamble Brook Falls	D, T, C	5, 6, 8 (15, 20, 25)	SP, F	B, RW	2 km (1.25 mi)	M-D	140	N
42. East River (Five Islands) Fall	D	8 (25)	SP	B, RW	1.5 km (0.9 mi)	M	140	N
43. North River (Five Islands) Fall	D	17 (55)	SP, F	T	1.25 km (0.8 mi)	M	80	N
44. Garden of Eden Fall	D	20 (65)	SP, F	B, T	1.2 km (0.75 mi)	D	105	N
45. McCarthy Gulch Falls	D, C, F	6, 11, 6, 8, 8 (20, 35, 20, 25, 25)	SP	B, RW	2.5 km (1.6 mi)	M	200	N
46. McCallum Gulch Falls	D, F	12, 9, 6, 8, 5 (40, 30, 20, 25, 15)	SP	B, RW	2 km (1.25 mi)	M-D	200	N
47. East Branch Moose River Fall	D, T, C, F	24 (80)	SP, F	B, RW	500 m/yd	D	150	N
48. West Branch Moose River Fall	D, T	14 (45)	SP, F	B, RW	300 m/yd	D	60	N
49. McAlese Brook Falls	D, T	12, 9, 12 (40, 30, 40)	SP, F	T, B, RW	2 km (1.25 mi)	D	300	N
50. Ripley's Fall	D, T	14 (45)	SP	R	250 m/yd	E	<20	Y
51. Wards Fall	D, S	6 (20)	SP, F	T	3.5 km (2.2 mi)	E	300	N
52. Horse Pasture Brook Falls	D, F	6, 6, 5 (20, 20 15)	SP	T, BW	2.5 km (1.6 mi)	E	120	Y
53. Wentworth Fall	F	11 (35)	SP, F	T	250 m/yd	E	<20	Y
54. Annandale Fall	D	14 (45)	SP	T	200 m/yd	D	25	Y
55. Arrowhead Fall	D	8 (25)	SP	B, RW	200 m/yd	M	<20	Y
SUNRISE TRAIL								
56. Four Mile Brook Falls	F	5, 12 (15, 40)	SP, F	RW	750 m/yd	M	40	Y
57. White Brook Fall	F	14 (45)	SP, F	B, RW	1 km (0.6 mi)	M	40	N
58. Fall Brook Fall (Sheepherders Junction)	S	12 (40)	SP, F	T	1.75 km (1.1 mi)	E	150	Y

Waterfall	Type	Height	Season	Access	Distance (one way)	Diff.	Elev.	Cell
59. Gairloch Brook Fall	T, C	14 (45)	SP	B, RW	500 m/yd	E-M	40	Y
60. Maple Brook Fall	C, T	11 (35)	SP, F	B, RW	1 km (0.6 mi)	E-M	60	Y
61. Glencoe Brook Fall	D, T	15 (50)	SP, F	R	250 m/yd	M	40	N
62. Black Brook (East River St. Marys) Fall	F	14 (45)	SP, F	T	200 m/yd	E	30	Y
63. Hurlbert Brook Fall	T, D	9 (30)	SP	B	200 m/yd	M	<20	Y
64. Polsons Brook Fall	T	5 (15)	SP	T	500 m/yd	E	<20	Y
65. Cuties Hollow Fall	D, T	14 (45)	SP, S, F	T	1.75 km (1.1 mi)	E	100	N
66. Vameys Brook Falls	D	4, 9 (13, 30)	SP, F	B, RW	1.75 km (1.1 mi)	M	140	N
MARINE DRIVE								
67. Johnson River Falls	T, C	3 (10)	SP, F	T, BW	2 km (1.25 mi)	E	<20	Y
68. Nuttall Brook Fall	D, T	6 (20)	SP, F	R	200 m/yd	E	<20	Y
69. Gleason Brook Fall	T	3, 6 (10, 20)	SP, F	B, RW	1 km (0.6 mi)	E	40	Y
70. Phantom Fall	T	11 (35)	SP, F	T	300 m/yd	E	30	N
71. Black Brook (Trafalgar) Fall	T, D	14 (45)	SP, F	BW	750 m/yd	E	80	N
72. Chisholm Brook Falls	D, T	3, 11, 11 (10, 35, 35)	SP, F	B, RW	1.75 km (1.1 mi)	M	200	N
73. Churn Brook Falls	D, T	6, 8, 6, 11 (20, 25, 20, 35)	SP, F	T, B, RW	2.5 km (1.6 mi)	M	150	N
74. Liscomb River Fall	D, S	9 (30)	YR	T	5 km (3.1 mi)	M	<20	N
75. Mira Falls (North Brook Falls)	D, T	12 (40)	SP, S, F	BW	1.5 km (0.9 mi)	M	80	Y
76. Hartley's Fall	S	8 (25)	SP	T, BW	100 m/yd	E	60	Y
MARCONI AND FLEUR DE LYS TRAILS								
77. MacCuishs Brook Fall	F	14 (45)	SP	B, RW	1 km (0.6 mi)	M	70	N
78. MacIsaacs Brook Falls	F	15 (50)	SP, F	B, RW	1.2 km (0.75 mi)	M	50	N
79. Gillis Brook Fall	D	6 (20)	SP, S, F	T	100 m/yd	E	<20	Y

Waterfall	Type	Height	Season	Access	Distance (one way)	Diff.	Elev.	Cell
80. St. Columba Fall	D	9 (30)	SP, F	R	100 m/yd	E	<20	Y
CEILIDH AND CABOT TRAILS								
81. Myles Doyle Fall	T	12 (40)	SP, F	R	100 m/yd	E	<20	Y
82. Second Branch Humes River Fall	D	15 (50)	SP, S, F	T, BW	5 km (3.1 mi)	M-D	300	Y
83. Black Brook (Middle River) Fall	D, T	15 (50)	SP, S, F	T	1 km (0.6 mi)	M	120	Y
84. MacRae Brook Falls	D, T, F	15 (50)	SP, F	B, RW	3 km (1.9 mi)	D-X	250	Y
85. Egypt Fall	T	18 (60)	SP, F	T	750 m/yd	M	100	Y
86. Tompkins Brook Fall	D, S	15 (50)	SP, F	B, RW	3 km (1.9 mi)	M	200	N
87. Bothan Brook Fall	S	15 (50)	SP	B, RW	1.5 km (0.9 mi)	M-D	200	N
88. Martha Brook Fall	D, S	23 (75)	SP, F	B	900 m/yd	X	120	N
89. Lavis Brook Falls	D, T, C	12 (40)	SP, F	T, B	1.5 km (0.9 mi)	E-M	100	N
90. Turner Brook Fall	F	30 (100)	SP, S, F	B, RW	1 km (0.6 mi)	X	200	N
91. Rocky Brook Fall	D, T, S	46 (150)	SP, S, F	B, RW	1.2 km (0.75 mi)	X	300	N
92. Factory Brook Fall	D, T, S	12 (40)	SP	B, RW	2.5 km (1.6 mi)	M	440	N
93. Farm Brook Fall	T, D	23 (75)	SP, F	T, RW	2.5 km (1.6 mi)	M	75	N
94. Fiset Brook Fall	T, D	18 (60)	SP, F	RW	1.5 km (0.9 mi)	D	80	N
95. Faribault Brook Fall	T, D	24 (80)	SP, S, F	T, B, RW	10 km (6 mi)	X	800	N
96. Goose Cove Brook Falls	S, T, D, C	8, 24, 18, 30 (25, 80, 60, 100)	SP, F	B, RW	3.5 km (2.2 mi)	M-D	250	N
97. North River Fall	D	30 (100)	YR	T	9 km (5.6 mi)	M	680	N
98. Timber Brook Fall	D	18 (60)	SP, F	T, BW	4 km (2.5 mi)	M	300	N
99. Great Falls	D	8 (25)	YR	T, BW	2.5 km (1.6 mi)	D-X	220	N
100. Pathend Brook Falls	S, D	6, 6, 15 (20, 20, 50)	SP, F	RW	2 km (1.25 mi)	M	130	Y

Lighthouse Route

The Lighthouse Route encompasses much of southwestern Nova Scotia. The route stretches from Halifax all the way to Yarmouth, hugging the Atlantic Ocean shoreline, and reaches north to the middle of Mainland Nova Scotia. This route probably has the fewest number of waterfalls in the province due to a lack of elevation, the presence of several dams on local rivers, and the geology prevalent in this area. Some of the falls included in this route would not have made the final list for other regions as they are not very high. However, their relative scarcity makes them worth a visit, as does their location near more densely populated parts of the province.

10. Broad River Falls

Lighthouse Route

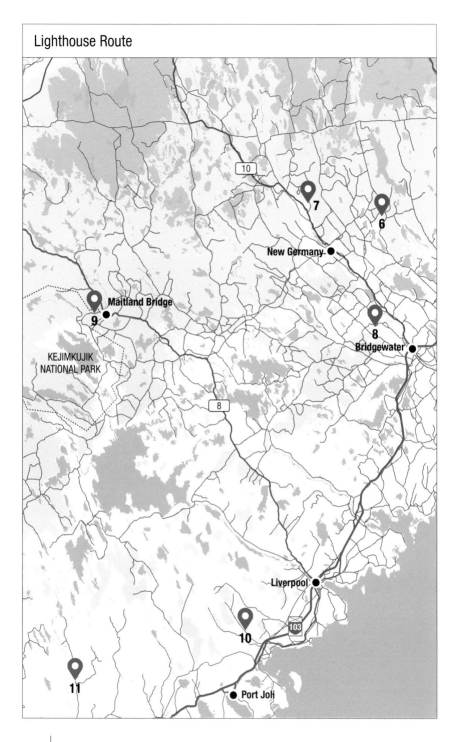

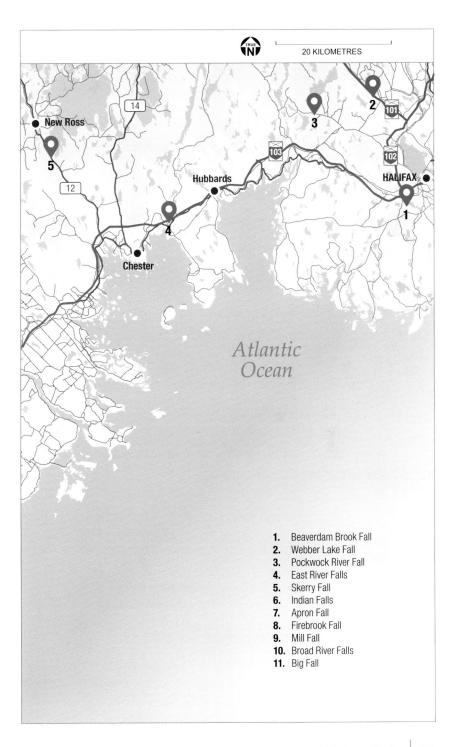

20 KILOMETRES

New Ross

14

5

12

Hubbards

103

3

2

101

102

HALIFAX

1

4

Chester

Atlantic Ocean

1. Beaverdam Brook Fall
2. Webber Lake Fall
3. Pockwock River Fall
4. East River Falls
5. Skerry Fall
6. Indian Falls
7. Apron Fall
8. Firebrook Fall
9. Mill Fall
10. Broad River Falls
11. Big Fall

1. Beaverdam Brook Fall

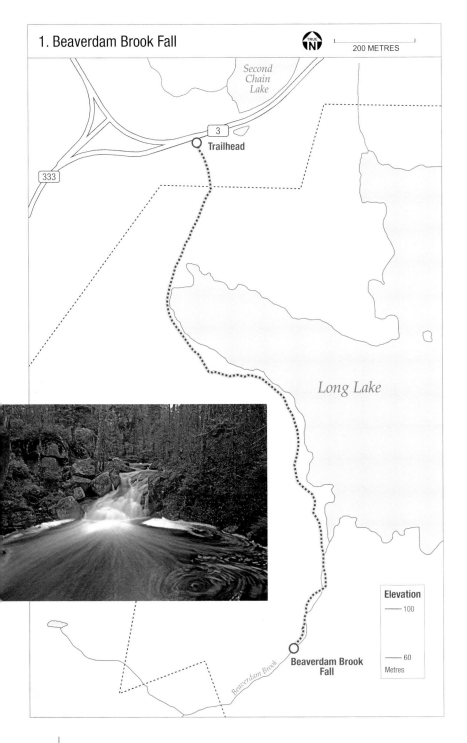

200 METRES

Second Chain Lake

3 Trailhead

333

Long Lake

Beaverdam Brook Fall

Beaverdam Brook

Elevation
—— 100

—— 60
Metres

1. Beaverdam Brook Fall

Type: Tiered
Height: 5 m (15 ft)
Best season(s): Spring and fall
Access: Trail
Source: Beaverdam Brook
Distance (one way): 1.5 km (0.9 mi)
Difficulty: Easy

Elevation: <20 m/yd
Hiking time: 30 minutes
Land ownership: Provincial Park
Maps: 11D12-Y3
Nearby waterfall(s): Quarry Brook Fall, Pockwock River Fall
Cellphone coverage: Y

Finding the trailhead: Take St. Margarets Bay Road/Highway 3 to the Long Lake Provincial Park parking lot, located east of the intersection of Highways 3 and 333. The trailhead starts at the parking lot. Trail contact info if necessary: Nova Scotia Provincial Parks: (902) 662-3030.

Trailhead: 44°37'55.3" N, 63°39'30.1" W   **Waterfall:** 44°37'16.6" N, 63°39'19.7" W

The hike: A few hundred metres/yards from one of Halifax's busiest areas lies Long Lake Provincial Park, a beautiful, partially hidden urban oasis. The 2,095 ha (5,176 ac) park, located just south of Bayer's Lake, was officially created in 1984. One of the lesser-known gems in this park is the waterfall located on Beaverdam Brook. The main fall is approximately 5 m (15 ft) high, making it one of the highest waterfalls in the Halifax area. The area upstream and downstream of the main waterfall has a few more scenic cascade-type drops. The forest around the fall is mixed with a few large evergreen specimens. The main fall has a large pool at the bottom, and a huge fallen tree crosses the small ravine in front of the fall.

From the parking lot, hike 300 m/yd to Long Lake following the brook. At the lake, hike to the west on a wide trail for approximately 300 m/yd. Before the trail starts to ascend a small hill, turn toward the lake on a secondary trail. Follow the trail that runs close to the edge of the lake until it leads to the outfall of Beaverdam Brook. Follow the brook upstream for a few hundred metres/yards to the main waterfall and cascades.

Bonus fall(s): There is a small fall off the Beechville-Lakeside-Timberlea (BLT) Trail in nearby Timberlea on Six Mile Lake Brook. Head east on the BLT Trail from where it crosses Clearwater Drive located off Highway 3.

2. Webber Lake Fall

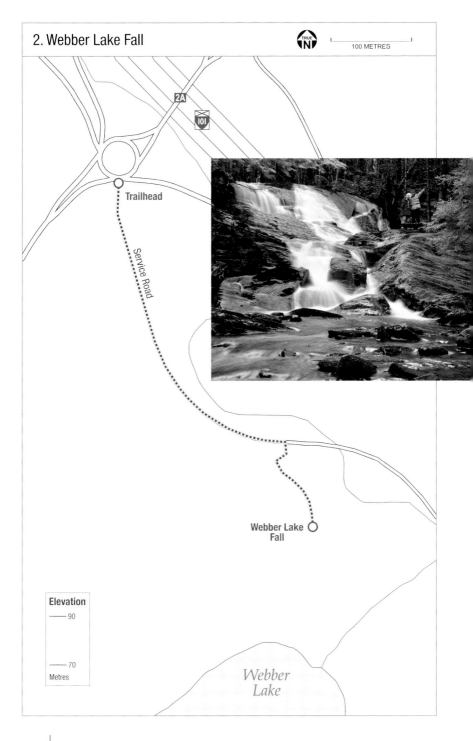

TRUE N
100 METRES

2A
101

Trailhead

Service Road

Webber Lake Fall

Elevation
—— 90

—— 70
Metres

Webber Lake

2. Webber Lake Fall

Type: Tiered
Height: 6 m (20 ft)
Best season(s): Spring and fall
Access: Trail
Source: Webber Lake
Distance (one way): 150 m/yd
Difficulty: Easy

Elevation: <20 m/yd
Hiking time: 20 minutes
Land ownership: Private
Maps: 11D13-X5
Nearby waterfall(s): Pockwock River Fall
Cellphone coverage: Y

Finding the trailhead: Take Exit 2A on Highway 101. On the west side of the highway there is a concrete barrier in the roundabout blocking vehicle access to Highway 101 Service Road, which parallels the highway. Walk 400 m/yd south on the Service Road to an area with a flooded pond on your left; the trailhead is on your right.

Trailhead: 44°46'45.44"N, 63°43'33.97"W   **Waterfall:** 44°46'43.47"N, 63°43'32.61"W

The hike: Webber Lake, located in the middle portion of the Sackville River watershed, is not an area that comes to mind when one is looking for a waterfall. Located only a few minutes from an exit on Highway 101, it remains largely unvisited. An earlier search for this waterfall as shown on a Sackville River Association map proved unsuccessful as there are two tributaries close to each other that feed Webber Lake, and I had followed the wrong one. I made a more triumphant visit on a rainy day during March break with my children.

From the trailhead, the fall is easy to find off an unofficial trail that bisects the stream. Just before the stream crossing there are some trees with red marks and a faint trail leading in a downstream direction. A short walk of 150 m/yd on this trail leads you through a softwood forest with a deep moss cover and ultimately in front of a nice two-tier fall of about 6 m (20 ft).

Bonus fall(s): From the bridge over the Sackville River by the Hefler Wood Plant, walk 200 m/yd downstream on the west side of the brook to a couple of small waterfalls and a fish ladder.

3. Pockwock River Fall

3. Pockwock River Fall

Type: Cascade
Height: 8 m (25 ft)
Best season(s): Year-round
Access: Trail
Source: Pockwock River
Distance (one way): 1 km (0.6 mi)
Difficulty: Easy

Elevation: 40 m/yd
Hiking time: 30 minutes
Land ownership: Private
Maps: 11D13-W5
Nearby waterfall(s): Webber Lake Fall
Cellphone coverage: Y

Finding the trailhead: From Highway 103, turn onto Hammonds Plains Road (Highway 213) for 13 km (8.1 mi). Turn onto Pockwock Road and park at the sharp bend located 5.6 km (3.5 mi) after the intersection with Highway 213. Continue as it becomes a gravel-based woods road. The trailhead is at the dirt road off the sharp bend on Pockwock Road.

Trailhead: 44°45'22.61"N, 63°51'22.32"W   **Waterfall:** 44°45'25.87"N, 63°52'4.57"W

The hike: The upper portion of the the Pockwock River watershed is protected as the water source for the Halifax Regional Municipality. However, the fall location does not lie in the protected area and therefore can be visited anytime. This is an easy hike that can be enjoyed by families to one of the tallest falls located within a few minutes from Halifax. The trail to the fall is mostly on the Old Pockwock Road, which in the past led to St. Margarets Bay. The 8 m (25 ft) fall is just 100 m/yd from this road off a well-worn path but is well hidden by the forest. There are a few large erratic boulders close to the river, and the waterfall is surrounded by a stand of mature evergreen trees. This waterfall can run almost dry in the summer, but the large pool at its base remains a welcome oasis for swimming during hot spells.

Follow the dirt road heading west to the fall, which is located 1 km (0.6 mi) away. The old road descends a moderate hill toward the Pockwock River. At the bottom of the hill and before the bridge over the river, turn right and follow the unofficial, 100 m/yd trail to the fall.

Bonus fall(s): On Hammonds Plain Road, turn onto Kearney Lake Road and then right onto Belle Street/Colins Road. Park at the cul-de-sac and hike on Hobsons Lake Trail. There is a series of small waterfalls downstream of the brook draining Hobsons Lake.

3. Pockwock River Fall

4. East River Falls - Chester

TRUE N

200 METRES

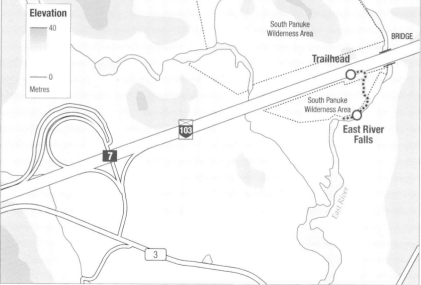

Elevation

— 40

— 0

Metres

South Panuke
Wilderness Area

BRIDGE

Trailhead

South Panuke
Wilderness Area

**East River
Falls**

103

7

East River

3

4. East River Falls

Type: Cascade
Height: 5 m (15 ft)
Best season(s): Spring, summer, and fall
Access: Roadside
Source: East River
Distance (one way): 200 m/yd
Difficulty: Easy

Elevation: <20 m/yd
Hiking time: 10 minutes
Land ownership: Crown
Maps: 21A09-Y4
Nearby waterfall(s): Indian Falls
Cellphone coverage: Y

Finding the trailhead: Take Highway 103 toward Chester. The highway crosses East River just before Exit 7 if you are heading west. Park at the bridge and head downstream. The trail starts right beside the sign indicating the distance to Hubbards and Halifax.

Trailhead: 44°35'44.60"N, 64°9'59.55"W   **Waterfall:** 44°35'39.64"N, 64°9'58.11"W

The hike: The little-known East River near Chester drains an area to the north of the falls that comes to within 1 km (0.6 mi) of Panuke Lake, which itself flows toward and into the Bay of Fundy. The area to the north of the waterfalls has been part of the South Panuke Wilderness Area since 2015. Thousands of vehicles drive by this hidden gem every day, but only a handful of people know about this location.

From the trailhead, a short hike of 200 m/yd leads you to two picturesque waterfalls amidst a grove of pine trees. Although these waterfalls are not very high, they can be quite impressive after a large rainfall. The first fall has a large square boulder set on its west side; the second fall is taller and has a deep pool at its base, and it practically begs to be run by a river kayak. The pool is also a perfect swimming spot in the summer months.

Bonus feature: A less-known feature to visit close to this waterfall is Labrador Castle. A trail to this rocky outcrop (44°36'21.4" N, 64°10'30.7" W) can be accessed off the Chester Connection Trail.

5. Skerry Fall

TRUE N

500 METRES

Skerry Fall

Gold River

Dirt Road

Trailhead

12

Seffern Lake Road

Elevation

180

100

Metres

Seffern Lake

5. Skerry Fall

Type: Cascade
Height: 5 m (15 ft)
Best season(s): Spring, summer, and fall
Access: Trail
Source: Gold River
Distance (one way): 2.5 km (1.6 mi)
Difficulty: Moderate

Elevation: 70 m/yd
Hiking time: 2 hours
Land ownership: Private and crown
Maps: 21A09-V2
Nearby waterfall(s): Indian Falls, East River Falls
Cellphone coverage: Y

Finding the trailhead: From Highway 103, take Highway 12 toward New Ross. Turn onto a dirt road on the west side of the highway, 450 m/yd north of Seffern Lake Road. Park on this dirt road, which leads all the way to the fall.

Trailhead: 44°41'14.60"N, 64°25'24.19"W   **Waterfall:** 44°41'11.28"N, 64°26'57.67"W

The hike: The Gold River, located in southwestern Nova Scotia, has a few waterfalls as it drains a large area from New Ross all the way to the Atlantic Ocean. Most of these falls are hard to access on foot as they are located in areas with few roads. Skerry Fall is easily accessible and among the most impressive of the falls, especially during the spring freshet. Downstream of the fall is a large and deep pool complete with a swinging rope attached to a large evergreen tree on the west side of the river. There is a large rocky outcrop on the east side of the fall that one can climb to get a bird's-eye view of the waterfall. The area to the south of this location is being considered for wilderness designation because of the presence of old hemlocks, red oaks, and white pines.

The dirt road is located only a few metres from the highway sign indicating New Ross. It is well used for the first half, and then it becomes overcrowded by evergreens and alders. Toward the end, it might disappear from view, but the sound of the waterfall (or your GPS) should guide you in the right direction.

Bonus fall(s): There is a small roadside fall located close by. Continue north on Highway 12, turn right on Lake Lawson Road, and drive to a stream crossing 900 m/yd further north. A small fall is to the right.

6. Indian Falls

TRUE N

200 METRES

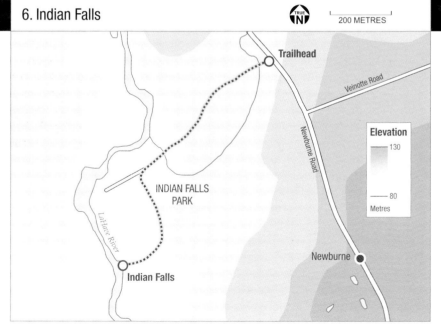

Trailhead

Veinotte Road

Newburne Road

INDIAN FALLS
PARK

LaHave River

Elevation

130

80
Metres

Indian Falls

Newburne

6. Indian Falls

Type: Slide
Height: 14 m (45 ft)
Best season(s): Spring and fall
Access: Trail
Source: North Branch LaHave River
Distance (one way): 200 m/yd
Difficulty: Easy

Elevation: <20 m/yd
Hiking time: 5 minutes
Land ownership: Municipal
Maps: 21A10-Y3
Nearby waterfall(s): Skerry Fall
Cellphone coverage: Y

Finding the trailhead: From Highway 103, take Exit 11 (Blockhouse) and drive north on Cornwall Road (Highway 324). Turn right onto Newburne Road and drive approximately 8 km/5 mi. Look for a sign on your left indicating Indian Falls Park. Turn and follow the directions to the parking area, located 750 m/yd from the intersection. Trail contact info if necessary: Municipality of the District of Lunenburg: (902) 542-8181.

Trailhead: 44°35'48.03"N, 64°35'54.90"W   **Waterfall:** 44°35'28.29"N, 64°36'17.08"W

The hike: The 90 km (56 mi) long LaHave River on the South Shore of Nova Scotia is one of the province's longest rivers and contains numerous varieties of waterfalls. Indian Falls on the North Branch of the LaHave River is one of those rare locations on the South Shore where a large fall remains undisturbed by a dam. The many waterfalls on the Mersey, LaHave, and Roseway Rivers have been disfigured by dams and all that is left are black-and-white pictures of those magnificent falls. The local government created a nature park at Indian Falls in 2004, so it is a perfect spot for a picnic (with privies) or a lazy afternoon spent on the rocky beach by the fall. The parking area is located a mere 200 m/yd from the waterfall. A short walk on a well-maintained trail through a stand of mature softwoods leads to the magnificent drop of the Indian Falls. There is a large outcrop of rock on the east side of the river between the forest and the fall that makes a perfect viewpoint to observe the fall. The fish passage on the west side of the river by the waterfall was reconstructed in the winter of 2017.

Bonus fall(s): Not far away, and just north of Stanburne, lies the Devil's Hook Falls. Follow the Stanburne Road north to where it crosses the North River and head 50 m/yd downstream of the bridge to the falls.

7. Apron Falls

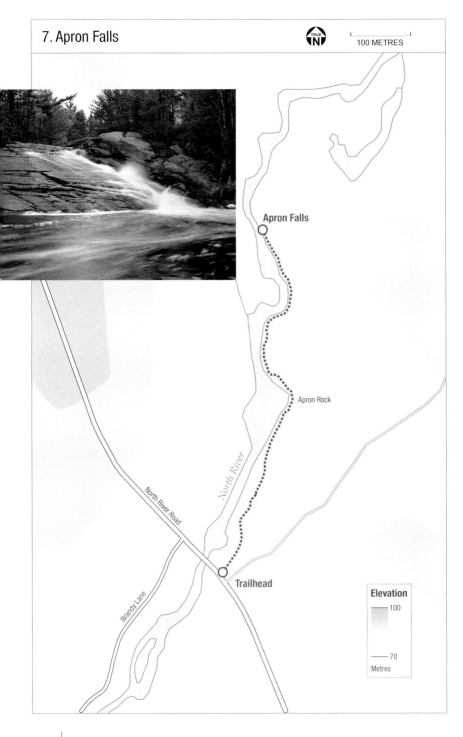

Apron Falls

Apron Rock

North River

North River Road

Brandy Lane

Trailhead

Elevation

—— 100

—— 70

Metres

7. Apron Falls

Type: Slide
Height: 8 m (25 ft)
Best season(s): Spring and fall
Access: Trail
Source: North River
Distance (one way): 1 km (0.6 mi)
Difficulty: Easy

Elevation: 30 m/yd
Hiking time: 30 minutes
Land ownership: Crown
Maps: 21A10-X3
Nearby waterfall(s): Firebrook Fall
Cellphone coverage: Y

Finding the trailhead: Take Highway 10 north from Bridgewater and turn right onto North River Road. Drive 1.7 km (1 mi) and park south of the bridge over North River. The trailhead can be found beside the bridge heading alongside the river in a northeasterly direction.

Trailhead: 44°36'29.57" N, 64°45'47.57" W   **Waterfall:** 44°36'45.42" N, 64°45'43.68" W

The hike: North River, located near Meisners Section, is a main tributary of the LaHave River. The river has numerous eye-catching names on the topographic maps such as Devil's Elbow, Whalesback Fall, James Fall, Devil Hook, and Apron Falls. Apron Falls is visible on satellite imagery as a long white ribbon set into the green forest.

Follow the small trail leading toward the river. A small fall of 1.2 m (4 ft) occurs within 100 m/yd of the trailhead with some large boulders and a granite ridge. Walking on the unofficial trail for 1 km (0.6 mi) leads you past some more interesting geology before you reach Apron Falls. This waterfall is unique for Nova Scotia. There is a large granitic rock slab that spans the whole width of the river. This large rock must be approximately 18.28 m (60 ft) across and 9.14 m (30 ft) high. When the water level is low, only a trickle of water can cross the granite, resulting in a 1-1.2 m (3-4 ft) deep meandering fall set within the rock face itself.

Bonus fall(s): Continue north on North River Road. Turn left onto Cherryfield Road. Park at the bridge over the LaHave River and walk downstream. There is a small fall here, and if you continue further downstream you will see the Zinc Spout .

200 METRES

8. Firebrook Fall

Type: Tiered
Height: 11 m (35 ft)
Best season(s): Spring and fall
Access: Roadside
Source: Wiles Lake Brook
Distance (one way): 200 m/yd
Difficulty: Easy

Elevation: <20 m/yd
Hiking time: 1 minute
Land ownership: Private
Maps: 21A07-Y2
Nearby waterfall(s): Apron Falls
Cellphone coverage: Y

Finding the trailhead: Take Highway 10 north from Bridgewater. Turn left onto Bruhm Road and follow it to its conclusion, 2.6 km (1.6 mi) away. Turn left onto Lower Branch Road. Turn immediately right onto Smith Road and park by a small bridge approximately 900 m/yd later. The falls are located south of Smith Road.

Trailhead: 44°25'39.20"N, 64°36'54.38"W   **Waterfall:** 44°25'38.42"N, 64°36'54.54"W

The hike: This is the most scenic and seldom visited fall near Bridgewater. The fall location is easy to find but remains well hidden from the road by a small stand of hardwoods. A previous trip down the road to Kayak Fall did not reveal to me this magnificent waterfall. The fall drops at least 11 m (35 ft) in numerous tiers with a change of direction between tiers. The shallow pool at the base is not suitable for swimming but does leave nice circles in time-lapse photos. The forest on either side is filled with evergreen trees protecting a deep layer of moss.

There is no official path to the fall. As soon as you exit your car and push through a hedge of small trees, you will be standing at the foot of the falls. At times of low water, one can walk within the brook and beside the falls. At times of high water, one will have to walk in the evergreen stand located on either side of the falls and peer from the 1.5-3 m (5-10 ft) ledges to the falls below if the view from the base is not satisfactory. Although this waterfall is located on the Little Wiles Lake Brook, the local name for it is Firebrook Fall, although it does not lie on Fire Brook, which is located a few kilometres away in Bakers Settlement.

Bonus fall(s): Continue on Upper Branch Road toward Bridgewater. Turn left on Forest View Drive. Park at the cul-de-sac and walk 900 m/yd on the ATV trail. A different and smaller ATV path goes toward the left and leads to a camping spot on the LaHave River. A mere 150 m/yd upstream of the camping area is a large set of rapids on the LaHave River called Frideaux Falls.

9. Mill Fall

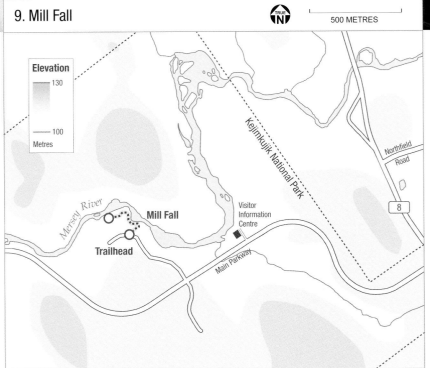

Elevation
130
100
Metres

Kejimkujik National Park

Northfield Road

Mersey River

Mill Fall

Visitor Information Centre

Trailhead

Main Parkway

8

500 METRES

9. Mill Fall

Type: Slide, drop
Height: 8 m (25 ft)
Best season(s): Spring and fall
Access: Trail
Source: Mersey River
Distance (one way): 200 m/yd
Difficulty: Easy

Elevation: <20 m/yd
Hiking time: 5 minutes
Land ownership: National Park
Maps: 21A06-X2
Nearby waterfall(s): Moose River Fall
Cellphone coverage: Y

Finding the trailhead: Take Highway 8 to Maitland Bridge. Enter Kejimkujik National Park and turn right onto Northfield Road, the second road on your right (the one after the Visitor Centre). Park at the end of the road, where the trailhead will be visible. Trail contact info if necessary: Kejimkujik National Park Visitor Centre: (902) 682-2772.

Trailhead: 44°26'9.25" N, 65°12'44.34" W   **Waterfall:** 44°26'19.84" N, 65°12'54.39" W

The hike: Mill Fall is located very close to the public entrance of Kejimkujik National Park. The park was established in the late 1960s, but the use of the many lakes within Kejimkujik dates back centuries, as evidenced by the Mi'kmaq petroglyphs found on slate outcrops. Mill Fall is named for the portable mill that was located at this location on the Mersey River more than a century ago. These days this area is protected as it lies within a national park.

The trailhead above is the shortest route to the fall among the multiple trails that lead there. From the parking area described above, a short 150 m/yd walk through a mature softwood stand leads to Mill Fall. This trail is well maintained, and the area round the fall may be crowded in the height of summer. The main fall is upstream of a large pond and there are some smaller falls downstream of the pond.

Bonus fall(s): Another set of (smaller) falls on the Mersey River is located at the Mersey River Chalets, located north of Maitland Bridge.

10. Broad River Falls

TRUE N

1000 METRES

Broad River Falls

Broad River

Dirt Road

Bonus Falls

103

Elevation

—— 100

—— 0

Metres

Trailhead

3

10. Broad River Falls

Type: Cascade
Height: 5 m (15 ft)
Best season(s): Spring
Access: Trail and bushwhack
Source: Broad River
Distance (one way): 4.5 km (2.1 mi)
Difficulty: Moderate

Elevation: 40 m/yd
Hiking time: 2 hours
Land ownership: Crown
Maps: 20P15-W1
Nearby waterfall(s): Big Fall
Cellphone coverage: N

Finding the trailhead: Broad River is the large river located between the White Point/Summerville and the Port Mouton exits on the new twinned section of Highway 103. Heading west on 103, a dirt road blocked by large stones is located 350 m/yd west of the bridge over the Broad River. Walk on this dirt road from Highway 103 for 4.5 km (2.1 mi) to a bridge over a tributary of the Broad River where the falls are located.

Trailhead: 43°57'16.06"N, 64°50'2.41"W   **Waterfall:** 43°58'31.97"N, 64°52'39.72"W

The hike: The Broad River is moderately long with a length of approximately 24 km (14.2 mi). Despite its name, it is not broader than most rivers of its size located in southwestern Nova Scotia. And although its waterfalls are not particularly tall, the relative scarcity of falls in this part of southwestern Nova Scotia makes them exceptional and worth a visit.

The walk on the 4.5 km (2.1 mi) dirt road is easy. Once you reach the bridge over this branch, a walk upstream or downstream along the brook leads to waterfalls. The walk to the downstream falls is not on a path but easy nonetheless as the tall evergreens overshadow most of the forest floor preventing the secondary growth of brush. The downstream fall is a cascading type of fall with numerous steps. The upstream fall is quite small and can be overlooked if time is in short supply, but it can be reached by following an ATV trail by the side of the river. These features would not qualify for falls in any other region of Nova Scotia but the geology present in this area prevents the development of any significantly taller falls.

Bonus fall(s): There are other small falls or rapids on the Broad River in an area just upstream of the bridge on old Highway 3 where it crosses the river.

11. Big Fall

TRUE N

500 METRES

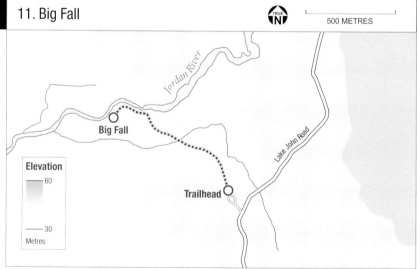

Jordan River

Big Fall

Lake John Road

Trailhead

Elevation
60

30
Metres

11. Big Fall

Type: Cascade
Height: 6 m (20 ft)
Best season(s): Spring
Access: Bushwhack
Source: Jordan River
Distance (one way): 1 km (0.6 mi)
Difficulty: Moderate

Elevation: <20 m/yd
Hiking time: 1 hour
Land ownership: Crown
Maps: 20P14-X2
Nearby waterfall(s): Broad River Falls
Cellphone coverage: N

Finding the trailhead: Take Highway 103 to Jordan Falls. Turn onto Lake John Road, drive 10 km (6.4 mi), and park approximately here: 43°53'39.26" N, 65°14'15.96" W. A small dirt road on the west side of Lake John Road is the general area where you should park. This road enters the wood and does a loop.

Trailhead: 43°53'37.91" N, 65°14'15.97" W   **Waterfall:** 43°53'54.89" N, 65°14'49.79" W

The hike: The Jordan River is one of the principal rivers of the South Shore of Nova Scotia, with a length of more than 60 km (37.5 mi). The river may be big, but the same cannot be said for its fall. In fact, Big Fall hardly qualifies as a fall; for this area, though, it's as big as they come. Most of the other falls nearby have been disfigured to harness hydro power, so this is actually a real hidden gem.

From the parking area, bushwhack in a straight line through some alder patches and pine forest sections. Some of the sections are quite nice to walk through as the brush is not very dense and the canopy is far overhead. In other sections, the pine trees are clumped together, making it more difficult to push through. After about 20 minutes of sustained effort you will reach the river. There is a trail by the side of the river marked by some orange flagging tape. This trail does not lead you back to the road but is rather a portage around the "Big Fall." Following the trail, there are a few small 1 m (2-3 ft) drops, and then the river bends and the biggest drop (about 2.4 m [8 ft] total) is in front of you.

Bonus fall(s): Drive west on Highway 3 to Shelburne. Turn onto Highway 203 North. The falls are on the Nova Scotia Power site to the left of that road just before you get to Riverview Drive.

Evangeline Trail

The Evangeline Trail includes the French Shore area near Meteghan, the Annapolis Valley, the Gaspereau Valley, and the area all the way east to Windsor. This trail area contains many waterfalls as it includes two important features; the North and South Mountains. These mountains lose roughly 215 and 275 metres (705 and 902 feet) of elevation respectively and are prone to the development of many waterfalls. This section could easily contain twice as many falls as listed in this guide, but the list was pared down to evenly span the whole area.

27. Black Hole Brook Fall

Evangeline Trail

12. Meteghan River Falls
13. Weymouth Falls
14. Walsh Brook Fall
15. Digby Gut Fall
16. Moose River Fall
17. Tupperville Brook Falls
18. St. Croix Fall
19. Eel Weir Brook Falls
20. Delanceys Brook Falls
21. Black River Falls

22. Crystal Fall
23. Shingle Mill Fall
24. Russia Road Brook Fall
25. Church Vault Brook Falls
26. Coby Irving Brook Fall
27. Black Hole Brook Fall
28. Moores Brook Fall
29. Little River Fall
30. Duncanson Brook Fall
31. Fall Brook Fall (Ettinger Fall)

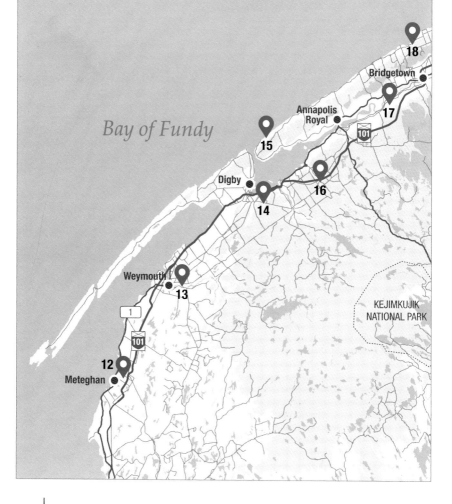

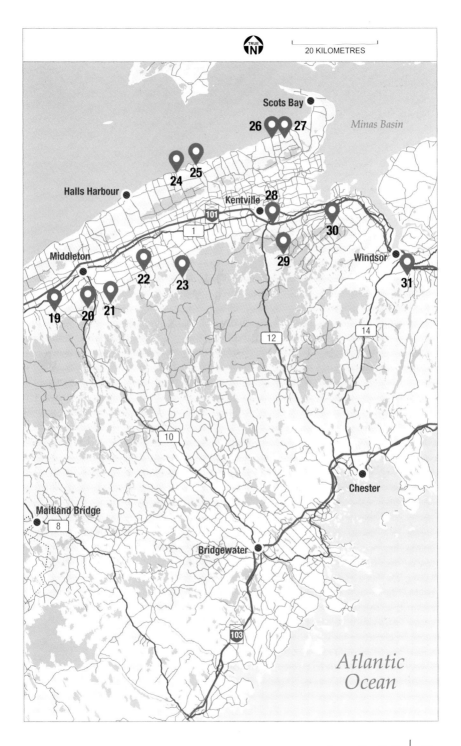

Scots Bay

Minas Basin

26 27

24 25

Halls Harbour

Kentville 28

101

1

30

Middleton

22 23

29

Windsor

19 20 21

31

12

14

10

Chester

Maitland Bridge

8

Bridgewater

103

Atlantic
Ocean

12. Meteghan River Falls

500 METRES

St. Marys Bay

Saulnier Road

Marc Comeau Road

Meteghan River

Placide Comeau Road

Elevation

30

0

Metres

101

Meteghan River

D'Entremont Road

Bonus Falls

Maillet Road

Moulin Road

Lower Fall

Middle Fall (Indian Fall)

Meteghan River Fall

Bangor Trailhead

1

Comeau Road

Comeau Branch

Ruisseau à Charles Black

St. Benoni

Marc Comeau Road

D'Entremont Road

12. Meteghan River Falls

Type: Cascade
Height: 2 m (6 ft)
Best season(s): Spring and fall
Access: Roadside
Source: Meteghan River
Distance (one way): 10 m/yd
Difficulty: Easy

Elevation: <5 m/yd
Hiking time: 5 minutes
Land ownership: Private
Maps: 21B01-Y1
Nearby waterfall(s): Weymouth Falls
Cellphone coverage: Y

Finding the trailhead: From Highway 1 in Meteghan, turn onto Marc Comeau Road. As the road crosses the bridge over the Meteghan River, the first fall can be found just downstream. The middle fall (Indian Falls) is located upstream from the bridge. The third fall can be visited by driving on Marc Comeau Road and then turning left onto Bangor Road. The fall is to the left of Bangor Road.

Trailhead: 44°12"50.8' N, 66°06"39.1' W   **Waterfall:** 44°12"52.1' N, 66°06"36.6' W

The hike: The Meteghan River is one of the main rivers draining the North Shore of Nova Scotia into St. Marys Bay. Before the river discharges into the bay, there are three falls located close to each other. The first one is best viewed at low tide and is located just downstream from the bridge on Marc Comeau Road. The second and tallest fall (Indian Falls) is absolutely gorgeous and can be viewed on the same bridge but looking upstream in the distance. The third fall is located upstream of the first two. The river at this spot drops approximately 2 m (7 ft) and has a large pool at its base that is framed by rocky outcrops on both sides. There is a swing rope over the river at this location, suggesting it is probably a well-used spot in the summer months.

Bonus fall(s): In the village of Meteghan River, turn onto D'Entremont Road and locate the falls downstream of the bridge over the Ruisseau à Charles Black.

13. Weymouth Falls

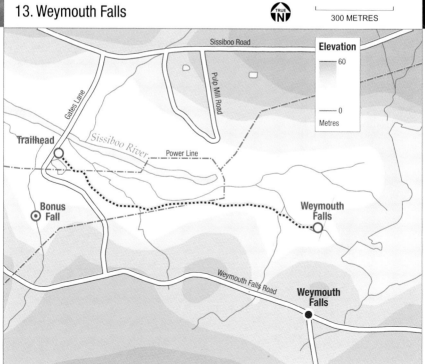

TRUE N

300 METRES

Sissiboo Road

Pulp Mill Road

Gates Lane

Elevation

60

0

Metres

Sissiboo River

Trailhead

Power Line

Bonus Fall

Weymouth Falls

Weymouth Falls Road

Weymouth Falls

13. Weymouth Falls

Type: Tiered
Height: 15 m (50 ft)
Best season(s): Spring
Access: Light bushwhack
Source: Sissiboo River
Distance (one way): 250 m/yd
Difficulty: Easy

Elevation: 30 m/yd
Hiking time: 15 minutes
Land ownership: Private and crown
Maps: 21A05-V2
Nearby waterfall(s): Indian Falls (Meteghan River)
Cellphone coverage: Y

Finding the trailhead: From Weymouth, continue south on Weymouth Falls Road for 4.2 km (2.6 mi) until you see the Gates Lane Road on your right. Turn onto Gates Lane Road and drive 600 m/yd to a metal bridge over the Sissiboo River. Park anywhere around here.

Trailhead: 44°24'11.35" N, 65°56'42.01" W   **Waterfall:** 44°24'19.74" N, 65°56'37.46" W

The hike: The origin of the name "Sissiboo" is either Mi'kmaq or French, meaning "river" or "six owls," respectively. There are currently three dams on the Sissiboo River that generate hydroelectricity. There are a few tracts of land protected as wilderness areas upstream of the Sissiboo Falls, which is located upstream of Weymouth Falls. A 15-minute hike along the west side of the river from a metal bridge downstream of the dam is required to reach Weymouth Falls. On top of the fall is a manufactured weir that, depending at the time of the year, will let water run to the fall or leave them dry.

From where you parked by the metal bridge, hike alongside the west side of the river heading upstream to the fall.

Bonus fall(s): A small brook flows from the hills on the west side of Gates Lane Road opposite the trailhead. Follow the brook upstream for 300 m/yd to a series of small falls and cascades.

14. Walsh Brook Fall

TRUE N

200 METRES

Walsh Brook
Fall

Walsh Brook

Lansdowne Road

Private Road

Trailhead

Private Road

Elevation

— 100

— 50

Metres

14. Walsh Brook Fall

Type: Tiered
Height: 8 m (25 ft)
Best season(s): Spring and fall
Access: Bushwhack
Source: Walsh Brook
Distance (one way): 250 m/yd
Difficulty: Moderate

Elevation: 30 m/yd
Hiking time: 15 minutes
Land ownership: Private
Maps: 21A12-X4
Nearby waterfall(s): Moose River Fall
Cellphone coverage: Y

Finding the trailhead: From Highway 101 to Digby, take Exit 25 and then Back Road (direction south) and turn right onto Lansdowne Road. Walsh Brook crosses the road 1.4 km (0.9 mi) after the turn. Park where you can. The fall is located downstream of the crossing.

Trailhead: 44°34'56.78"N, 65°43'36.85"W   **Waterfall:** 44°35'5.82"N, 65°43'36.88"W

The hike: Walsh Brook is a 5 km (3.1 mi) long brook that bisects the plateau between the deep valleys of the Bear River and Acacia Brook south of Digby. The waterfall on Walsh Brook is not very well known and seldom visited. Many thanks to "Riverwalker" J. Riley for graciously sharing this out-of-the-way fall.

The hike starts in an alder patch but soon joins a semi-established path. The path leads to an immature evergreen forest. Once in the forest, the sound of the falls is prevalent. The terrain begins to slope downward and then reaches a rocky knife's edge. The fall is to your right. From this point, the terrain becomes pretty vertical and the moss-covered ground can be very slippery, so extra caution is advised to get to the bottom.

Bonus fall(s): Head to the Acacia Valley trails system. There is a fall off one of the main trails. This is located off Mill Road, which can be accessed via Ridge Road in nearby Hillgrove.

15. Digby Gut Fall

TRUE N

300 METRES

Kettle Fall

Main Fall

Smaller Falls

Bay of Fundy

Dirt Road

Elevation
100

0

Metres

Trailhead

Granville Road

Dirt Road

15. Digby Gut Fall

Type: Drop, cascade, slide
Height: 8 m (25 ft)
Best season(s): Spring
Access: Shore and river walking, bushwhack
Source: Fleet Brook
Distance (one way): 3.5 km (2.2 mi)

Difficulty: Moderate
Elevation: 150 m/yd
Hiking time: 3 hours
Land ownership: Private and crown
Maps: 21A12-X1
Nearby waterfall(s): Walsh Brook Fall
Cellphone coverage: N

Finding the trailhead: In Port Royal, take Granville Road due west for 15.5 km (9.6 mi) to Victoria Beach. In Victoria Beach and at the intersection of Everett Mountain Road, continue on Granville Road for 4.6 km (2.9 mi) as it becomes a dirt road with lots of potholes until a ninety-degree turn at 44°42'40.3" N, 65°44'20.3" W. Park your car there or before if you do not have enough clearance.

Trailhead: 44°42'9.11" N, 65°44'49.98" W   **Waterfall:** 44°43'2.14" N, 65°43'34.29" W

The hike: Although Fleet Brook doesn't flow into Digby Gut, the unnamed falls were close enough to this main geographical feature to warrant the name. Fleet Brook is only approximately 3 km (1.9 mi) long and flows just due east of Digby Gut. However, the lack of length doesn't prevent the formation of numerous waterfalls as this brook loses almost 152 m (500 ft) of elevation on its way from the top of the North Mountain into the Bay of Fundy.

A nice hike along the shore of the Bay of Fundy for about 1.5 km (0.9 mi) leads to the unassuming Fleet Brook, which has three major falls and countless smaller falls and sliders. The hike along the seashore is a bit difficult at first but gets easier as you approach Fleet Brook. Once you are at the brook, there is a 5 m (17 ft) kettle fall, so named because it has a huge boulder in its middle section. The main fall is just a bit further upstream, and it is a cascading type. Its many small steps make it seem taller than it actually is. Further upward lie a few more falls of 1–3 m (3.5–10 ft) in height until you intersect a dirt road located 1.5 km (0.9 mi) away from the seashore. Use this dirt road to get back quickly to the starting point.

Bonus fall(s): Another fall is located on the shoreline off an unofficial path that you can locate on the dirt road 1.15 km (0.7 mi) after the pavement ends. At this point you should pass over a small bridge with your car and the road is quite wide in this area. A small trail to the northeast of the bridge leads to the beach and the fall.

16. Moose River Fall

TRUE N

100 METRES

101

Moose River

Quarry Road

Clementsport Road

Trailhead

Elevation
110

80
Metres

**Moose River
Fall**

16. Moose River Fall

Type: Tiered
Height: 6 m (20 ft)
Best season(s): Spring
Access: Trail
Source: Moose River
Distance (one way): 100 m/yd
Difficulty: Easy

Elevation: <20 m/yd
Hiking time: 2 minutes
Land ownership: Private
Maps: 21A12-Z3
Nearby waterfall(s): Walsh Brook Fall
Cellphone coverage: Y

Finding the trailhead: Take Highway 1 to Clementsport. Turn onto Clementsport Road and follow it until you drive under Highway 101. Turn left onto Quarry Road and park at the bridge over Moose River. The fall is hidden just upstream of the bridge.

Trailhead: 44°37'46.80" N, 65°33'46.01" W   **Waterfall:** 44°37'44.92" N, 65°33'47.34" W

The hike: The Moose River, located near Digby, is not easily mistaken for the larger East Branch and West Branch Moose Rivers located across the Bay of Fundy near Parrsboro. The Moose River located on the Evangeline Trail, although 13 km (8 mi) in length, just doesn't carry the same volume of water, neither has it carved the deep valleys located in the Cobequid Hills. Regardless, this is a pretty falls, and it is tucked away just far enough from Highway 101 that it remains mostly unvisited.

The hike to the fall is very short and easy through a mixed forest. The falls are broad and offer a small oasis. Since the hike is short, it is not a destination hike but rather a great place to stretch your legs or have a picnic.

Bonus fall(s): Driving east on Highway 1, just before you turn onto Clementsport Road you will cross over a small brook. Some 50 m/yd before you cross the brook, keep your eyes open for a faint trail that leads up a steep slope and onto a private property. The homeowners welcome hikers, but do ask their permission. Follow the trail upstream to the fall, approximately 800 m/yd away.

17. Tupperville Brook Falls

TRUE N

100 METRES

201

Tupperville
Community
Hall

Bent Brook

Trailhead

Farm
Buildings

Power Line

Tupperville

Brook

Elevation

110

80

Metres

**Tupperville Brook
Falls**

17. Tupperville Brook Falls

Type: Cascade, tiered
Height: 15 m (50 ft)
Best season(s): Spring
Access: Trail
Source: Tupperville Brook
Distance (one way): 1.25 km (0.8 mi)
Difficulty: Easy

Elevation: 140 m/yd
Hiking time: 30 minutes
Land ownership: Private
Maps: 21A14-W5
Nearby waterfall(s): St. Croix Fall, Moose River Fall
Cellphone coverage: Y

Finding the trailhead: Take Highway 201 to Tupperville and turn left onto a dirt road that is located beside a wooden building at 44°47'44.9" N, 65°22'17.3" W. The dirt road is located approximately 750 m/yd west, past the second entrance to Tupperville Road. The Tupperville Community Hall is next to the road. You can see some orchards just past the buildings. Continue for 440 m/yd to a Y intersection. Turn left and drive a further 220 m/yd to the entrance to farm buildings surrounded by a fence located to your right. Park there, taking care not to block the farm road.

Trailhead: 44°47'43.70" N, 65°22'17.40" W   **Waterfall:** 44°47'12.07" N, 65°21'28.93" W

The hike: Tupperville Brook drains a section of the South Mountain in an area located near Bridgetown. Although it loses 250 m/yd of elevation from the mountains to the Annapolis River, most of the waterfalls are located close to the Annapolis River. This is a good family-friendly trail to some spectacular waterfalls near Bridgetown. The sound of the falls becomes more prevalent once you pass a small camp by the side of the trail. The first part of the falls consists mostly of cascades over and under big boulders. A hike further upstream leads to another and bigger fall that runs on top of the rock face. The last fall, which is the tallest, looks like a waterslide.

Keep the fence on your left and follow the ATV path up the hill. After crossing a small brook on the trail, you should hear the falls located on the left-hand side of the trail. The map shows the small bushwhack required to reach the fall and subsequently return to the ATV path.

Bonus fall(s): In nearby Round Hill, turn on an unnamed road running south almost opposite Wharf Road. Continue until the road ends at a quarry. Park there and bushwhack to the river and a small fall upstream.

18. St. Croix Fall

TRUE N

200 METRES

Bay of Fundy

Poole Brook

Shore Road East

St. Croix Fall

Trailhead

Elevation

90

0

Metres

18. St. Croix Fall

Type: True drop
Height: 14 m (45 ft)
Best season(s): Spring, fall, and winter
Access: Trail
Source: Poole Brook
Distance (one way): 150 m/yd
Difficulty: Easy to moderate

Elevation: 40 m/yd
Hiking time: 10 minutes
Land ownership: Private
Maps: 21A14-W2
Nearby waterfall(s): Tupperville Brook Falls
Cellphone coverage: N

Finding the trailhead: In Bridgetown, take Hampton Mountain Road toward Valley View Provincial Park. Continue on Hampton Mountain Road and then turn right onto Shore Road. Drive for approximately 3 km (1.9 mi) and park.

Trailhead: 44°54'58.19" N, 65°18'12.33" W   **Waterfall:** 44°55'0.22" N, 65°18'18.43" W

The hike: Poole Brook Fall is also known as St. Croix Cove Fall, and it is one of the most scenic waterfalls in mainland Nova Scotia. The hike is not long or strenuous, but it does require some effort as the trail loses more than 76 m (250 ft) in elevation over its length. At this particular location, Poole Brook has a true drop of about 14 m (45 ft) into a small gorge. The forest is a mixture of mature conifers and leafy trees. Once in the forest, the roar of the fall drowns all other woodland sounds. The trail is easy enough for children, but the descent into the small gorge is quite steep for a short length. At the bottom there is a small pool, but it seems very shallow for swimming. The fall stands impressively in front of you, and you can even go behind it to look for some hidden treasure!

Near where you parked, there is a small path, located on the east side of the brook, which leads downstream. This small unofficial trail leads all the way to the base of the fall.

Bonus feature: Walk all the way downstream and head east on the Fundy shoreline to some high cliffs and a chance to do some mineral hounding.

19. Eel Weir Brook Falls

TRUE N

200 METRES

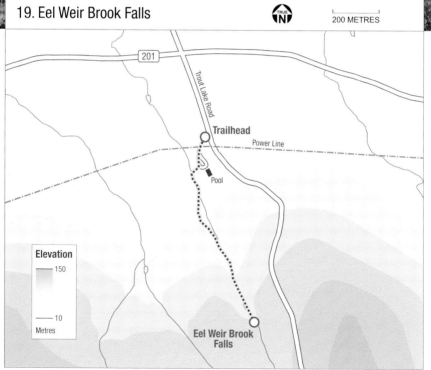

201

Trout Lake Road

Trailhead

Power Line

Pool

Elevation

150

10

Metres

Eel Weir Brook
Falls

19. Eel Weir Brook Falls

Type: Drop, tiered
Height: 12 m (40 ft)
Best season(s): Spring
Access: River walking
Source: Eel Weir Brook
Distance (one way): 1.1 km (0.7 mi)
Difficulty: Moderate

Elevation: 85 m/yd
Hiking time: 1 hour
Land ownership: Private
Maps: 21A14-Y3
Nearby waterfall(s): St. Croix Fall, Tupperville Brook Falls
Cellphone coverage: N

Finding the trailhead: Take Exit 18 on Highway 103. Turn left onto Elliot Road and drive 2.3 km (1.4 mi) to Highway 1. Turn left onto Highway 1 and drive 700 m/yd and turn right onto Lawrencetown Lane. Continue straight on Lawrencetown Lane for 900 m/yd. Drive straight through at the Highway 201 intersection. Lawrencetown Lane is here renamed Trout Lake Road. Drive to the swimming pool road located on the right, 400 m/yd after crossing Highway 201.

Trailhead: 44°52'19.2"N, 65°09'09.2"W   **Waterfall:** 44°51'53.7"N, 65°08'59.3"W

The hike: This hike leads into the woods and up the South Mountain located near West Lawrencetown, Annapolis County. There are at least seven waterfalls to observe during this hike. The brook coming down the South Mountain loses a lot of elevation, but due to the geology of the area instead of creating one massive waterfall, the brook has multiple falls of 1.5-3 m (5-10 ft) in height. The exception to this rule is the Eel River Brooks Falls.

Walk by the swimming pool and head toward the brook. Follow the brook upstream and through a magnificent and mature evergreen forest. Within the brook and on the side of the ravine are lots of boulders, which are fun to climb over as you walk upstream to see the next waterfalls. The first time I explored this brook, I wasn't aware of the massive fall on this brook and stopped hiking approximately 200 m/yd short of it. On a subsequent visit to this site and hiking from a different direction, I encountered the topmost fall. The fall and the rocky outcrops block the entire upstream end of the ravine, and large boulders have fallen on the side and in the brook at the foot of the waterfall. This is truly a spectacular fall.

Bonus fall(s): There are a few smaller, slider-type falls on Petes Brook, located 1.9 km (1.2 mi) east of Trout Lake Road on Highway 201.

20. Delanceys Brook Falls

TRUE N

200 METRES

Delanceys Brook Falls

Trailhead

Elevation
180
130
Metres

Dirt Road

Inglisville Road

Delanceys Brook

20. Delanceys Brook Falls

Type: Tiered, cascade
Height: 2, 5, 5 m (6, 15, 15 ft)
Best season(s): Spring and fall
Access: Bushwhack and river walking
Source: Delanceys Brook
Distance (one way): 500 m/yd
Difficulty: Easy (no trail)

Elevation: 20 m/yd
Hiking time: 15 minutes
Land ownership: Crown
Maps: 21A14-Z3
Nearby waterfall(s): Eel Weir Brook Falls, Black River Falls
Cellphone coverage: N

Finding the trailhead: Take Highway 10 south from Middleton for 13.2 km (8.2 mi). Turn right onto Alpena Road for 3.4 km (2.1 mi), then right onto Inglisville Road. Inglisville Road becomes a dirt road and then branches in a few directions. Keep on the main branch until you reach Delanceys Brook, 5.4 km (3.4 mi) away. The road can be driven all the way to Delanceys Brook with a high-clearance vehicle.

Trailhead: 44°52'21.81"N, 65°03'6.84"W   **Waterfall:** 44°52'29.9"N, 65°03'09.9"W

The hike: The waterfalls on this brook were found by reading an old and preliminary geological map of the Torbrook mining district (Roberts et al., 1905). No other recent sources of information were found on the possibility of waterfalls on this brook. However, a brief look at the satellite imagery in the vicinity of the potential fall location showed a large opening in the canopy over the brook. Furthermore, there was even a logging road within 500 m/yd of this feature, so I reckoned an exploration hike to it would be easy.

A short and easy walk on the side of the brook by some small cascades eventually leads to the hole in the canopy. There is a small slide fall here but only of about 2 m (6 ft). However the large pool is surrounded on one side by a unique rock formation. Looking further downstream, there is another opening in the forest. A walk of 50 m/yd leads, surprisingly, to two separate falls created by the splitting of the brook into two branches.

Bonus feature: Upstream of the dam on the Nictaux River are the Alpena Rapids. They can be reached via a dirt road located across from the intersection of Alpena Road and Highway 10.

21. Black River Falls

TRUE
N

200 METRES

Elevation
200
110
Metres

Black River
Falls

Meadow Brook

Trailhead
Quarry

Black River

Bloomington Road

Allen Lake Road

Bloomington

21. **Black River Falls**

Type: Tiered, cascade
Height: 5, 3, 6 m (15, 10, 20 ft)
Best season(s): Spring
Access: Bushwhack and river walking
Source: Black River
Distance (one way): 1 km (0.6 mi)
Difficulty: Easy to moderate (no trail)

Elevation: 40 m/yd
Hiking time: 1 hour
Land ownership: Nature Reserve
Maps: 21A15- V3
Nearby waterfall(s): Crystal Fall
Cellphone coverage: N

Finding the trailhead: From Highway 10 near Nictaux Falls, turn onto Torbrook Road, then turn onto Bloomington Road. Drive 2.6 km (1.6 mi) south and turn onto Allen Lake Road. Take two sharp bends on Allen Lake Road, cross the Black River, and at the next sharp bend is the location of a quarry. Park here.

Trailhead: 44°53'03.3"N, 64°58'58.0"W   **Waterfall:** 44°53'16.5"N 64°59'24.4"W

The hike: The opportunity to explore this river materialized after reading the Roberts et al. (1905) map of the area, which indicated a few waterfalls on the Black River and on a nearby tributary. Again, no other source of information confirmed the presence of waterfalls in this area. I observed two distinct falls on the tributary, but the water level was too low to appreciate them. Upon reaching the Black River, it was abundantly evident why this area is protected as a 144 ha (356 ac) nature preserve. The area near the Black River offers some fine examples of old and mature Red and White Pines as well as Eastern Hemlocks and White Ash. A short section of the river offers a series of four magnificent falls. The first one even splits into two sides of a small island. There were minimal signs of human activity when I visited, but I think this spot remains mostly unvisited.

From where you parked, the hike begins with a short walk on an increasingly alder-choked dirt road. Upon reaching a small tributary, the hike continues into the woods and follows the tributary down a ravine and toward its confluence with the Black River.

Bonus fall(s): There is a large waterfall at the dam site on the Nictaux River approximately at 44°51'13.3" N, 65°01'37.9" W. However, the fall can run dry at certain times of the year.

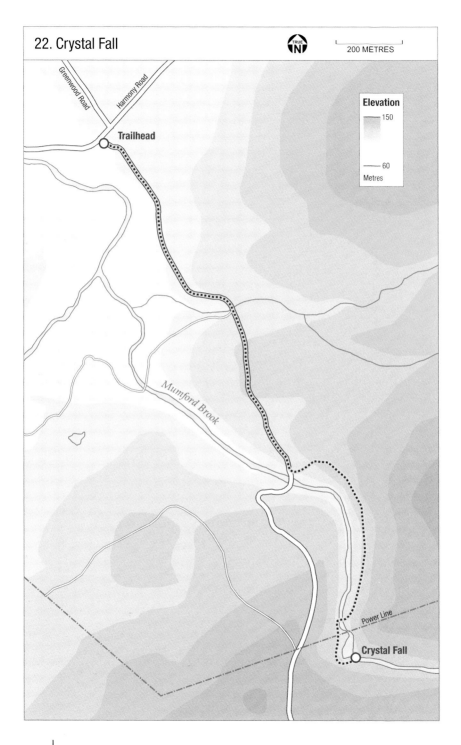

22. Crystal Fall

TRUE N

200 METRES

Elevation
150

60
Metres

Greenwood Road

Harmony Road

Trailhead

Mumford Brook

Power Line

Crystal Fall

22. Crystal Fall

Type: Drop
Height: 8 m (25 ft)
Best season(s): Spring and fall
Access: Trail
Source: Mumford Brook
Distance (one way): 2 km (1.25 mi)
Difficulty: Easy

Elevation: 160 m/yd
Hiking time: 1 hour
Land ownership: Private and crown
Maps: 21A15-W2
Nearby waterfall(s): Shingle Mill Fall
Cellphone coverage: Y

Finding the trailhead: From Highway 1 east of Kingston, take Highway 201 and follow it for 6.6 km (4.1 mi) toward South Greenwood. Turn left onto Greenwood Road for 900 m/yd and then right onto Meadowvale Road for 120 m/yd and immediately left again on Greenwood Road (again). Drive 1.3 km (0.8 mi) to Harmony Road. Turn right onto Harmony Road and drive 50 m/yd to the dirt road on your left, which is the trailhead. Park here.

Trailhead: 44°57'0.14" N, 64°53'17.30" W   **Waterfall:** 44°56'15.63" N, 64°52'41.89" W

The hike: Mumford Brook and the Fales River combine in an area to the south of Greenwood to form one of the main tributaries of the Annapolis River. Crystal Fall on Mumford Brook has a deep pool in front of it and significant rocky cliffs on the eastern side. The western side of the fall and its approach are set into a mature evergreen forest. A trail has been developed unofficially all around the fall but there are no bridges to cross the river close to the fall. Logs are regularly placed and lashed down together to help people cross the river.

The first part of the trail is wide enough and smooth enough that most people will drive a way down the road to a washed-out culvert. The whole way to the fall is under a mature evergreen forest, and you hear the sound of the water from the river almost the whole time you are hiking. Approximately 1.25 km (0.8 mi) from Harmony Road, a bridge appears to the right. Do not turn toward the bridge but continue straight on the dirt path. After just a short elevation gain, a secondary trail appears on your right. Follow it all the way to the fall.

Bonus falls: There is another great set of falls on the same river. This series of falls is located just downstream of the metal bridge over the Fales River that you will see as you drive west on the Harmony Road from the trailhead.

23. Shingle Mill Fall

Type: Tiered
Height: 6 m (20 ft)
Best season(s): Spring, summer, and fall
Access: Trail
Source: South Brook
Distance (one way): 1 km (0.6 mi)
Difficulty: Easy

Elevation: 40 m/yd
Hiking time: 45 minutes
Land ownership: Crown
Maps: 21A15-X2
Nearby waterfall(s): Crystal Fall
Cellphone coverage: Y

Finding the trailhead: From Highway 101, take the Berwick exit to Highway 1. Drive west on Highway 1 to Aylesford East and take a left turn onto Aylesford Road toward Factorydale. Drive 11 km (6.8 mi) up the South Mountain to a well-used logging road on your right and turn onto it at 44°57.024' N, 64°44.049' W. Drive 3.8 km (2.4 mi) to another dirt road on your left that is heading south.

Trailhead: 44°56'20.78" N, 64°46'24.17" W   **Waterfall:** 44°55'52.12" N, 64°46'11.01" W

The hike: The water running in the Shingle Mill Fall originates in the two main reservoirs on top of the South Mountain near Aylesford. An area to the south of the Burnt Dam Flowage Reservoir shows a waterfall named Shingle Mill Fall on the topographical maps. The roar of Shingle Mill Fall is heard before the fall comes into view on the right side of a dirt road. This is not the tallest fall in the area, but it remains a beautiful sight tucked away in a small depression. The fall drops into two main tiers under a mostly mature leafy forest. Getting to the waterfall in winter using snowshoes or cross-country skis is a definite possibility at this location. A brief reconnaissance around the fall did not reveal any signs of the old shingle mill.

The trail to the fall is on a dirt road that was being used for logging in the fall of 2016. There were large trucks on the road, so be careful. Follow the main road in a southerly direction for approximately 1 km (0.6 mi).

Bonus fall(s): Drive on Aylesford Road south all the way to Forties Road. Turn left on Forties Road and drive 3.8 km (2.4 mi) to a bridge over the Sherbrooke River. There are a few cascade-type falls downstream of that bridge.

23. Shingle Mill Fall

TRUE N

500 METRES

Aylesford Road

Dirt Road

Trailhead

South River

Shingle Mill
Fall

Burnt
Dam
Flowage

Elevation

— 230

— 170

Metres

24. Russia Road Brook Fall

TRUE N

200 METRES

Bay of Fundy

Russia Road
Brook Fall

Russia Road Brook

Bonus
Fall

Bear Brook

Trailhead

Elevation

60

0

Metres

Russia Road

Spicer Road

360

24. Russia Road Brook Fall

Type: True drop
Height: 9 m (30 ft)
Best season(s): Spring
Access: Shore walking
Source: Unnamed brook
Distance (one way): 800 m/yd
Difficulty: Easy

Elevation: <20 m/yd
Hiking time: 45 minutes
Land ownership: Crown
Maps: 21H02-X2
Nearby waterfall(s): Church Vault Brook Falls
Cellphone coverage: N

Finding the trailhead: On Highway 101, take Exit 15 and turn right onto Highway 360 toward Harbourville. Continue on this road for 12.2 km (7.6 mi) as it climbs the North Mountain and then descends toward the Bay of Fundy. Turn right onto Russia Road and drive about 700 m/yd. You should see a dirt road on your left. Park here.

Trailhead: 45°9'4.96" N, 64°47'49.98" W   **Waterfall:** 45°9'18.81" N, 64°47'40.91" W

The hike: Any significant walk on the shoreline of the Bay of Fundy will eventually lead to some waterfalls. This hike will take you to an area that is lined with 30 m (100 ft) cliffs and two waterfalls. This hike is not possible at high tides. The cliffs are orange and pink in colour and quite scenic with lots of pockets of minerals throughout. Across the water you will notice Cape Chignecto, Cape D'Or, and Ile Haute. There are a few sea caves worth the detour located to the east of the fall, and in winter there is the possibility of ice climbing.

To get to the fall, simply follow the dirt road down to the beach. Turn right and continue to the fall. Due to the 12 m (40 ft) high tides in the Bay of Fundy, the hike takes place on the seafloor at low tide, hence the appearance of a path in the water on the map.

Bonus fall(s): On the beach accessed via the trailhead, there is the 2 m (6 ft) Bear Brook Fall. You will need to check tides before you set off as the whole route is lined by cliffs that have their base underwater at high tide. Once you are on the shoreline, a hike of 800 m/yd due east leads you to the waterfall, which plunges dramatically into the sea.

25. Church Vault Brook Falls

TRUE N

200 METRES

Bay of Fundy

Black Rock Road

Canada Creek

Wharf

Wall Street

Trailhead

Canada Creek North Br

Church Vault

Church Vault
Brook Falls

Black Rock Road

Brook

Elevation

50

0

Metres

25. Church Vault Brook Falls

Type: Drop, cascade, tiered
Height: 6 m (20 ft)
Best season(s): Spring and fall
Access: River walking
Source: Church Vault Brook
Distance (one way): 500 m/yd
Difficulty: Easy

Elevation: 30 m/yd
Hiking time: 1 hour
Land ownership: Private
Maps: 21H02-X2
Nearby waterfall(s): Russia Road Brook Fall
Cellphone coverage: Y

Finding the trailhead: On Highway 101, take Exit 15 and turn right onto Highway 360. Drive 12.2 km (7.6 mi) up the North Mountain toward Harbourville. Turn right onto Russia Road for 3.3 km (2 mi) and then left onto Black Rock Road. Drive 3.4 km (2 mi) to Canada Creek. Church Vault Brook is located in Canada Creek and flows into the small protected harbour on the left. Park near here.

Trailhead: 45°10'12.38" N, 64°44'35.33" W   **Waterfall:** 45°10' 3.93" N, 64°44' 35.84" W

The hike: The majority of people who drive in this region are in awe of the scenic seashore views, but most of them are oblivious to the treasures hidden along the brooks that are actively carving the North Mountain. A short hike of about 500 m/yd beside the Church Vault Brook in Canada Creek leads you to a series of beautiful waterfalls. There are two main falls of about 3-6 m (10-20 ft), but don't let the height deter you from visiting as these falls are well worth the trip. The forest near the falls is a mixture of evergreen and deciduous trees. This is a nice little stroll to do when you are passing in the area and do not have enough time to venture out for a longer hike.

From the parking spot, hike the brook upstream. Once you reach the bridge, hike on the western side of the brook and beat your way through small underbrush until you reach the forest with a high tree canopy. A short hike of 5 minutes takes you to the first fall. The next few waterfalls upstream can be viewed from the top of the first fall.

Bonus fall(s): On Highway 360 just after cresting the North Mountain, turn left on Barley Street and park 600 m/yd down the road by a small bridge. Hike downstream to an impressive 9 m (30 ft) slider fall.

26. Coby Irving Brook Fall

TRUE N

|———————| 200 METRES

Bay of Fundy

Caroline Cove

Dirt Road

Coby

Bigelow Cove Road

Black Hole Brook

**Coby
Irving Brook
Fall**

Irving Brook

Trailhead

Old Baxter Mill Road

Elevation

— 60

— 0

Metres

26. Coby Irving Brook Fall

Type: Drop
Height: 12 m (40 ft)
Best season(s): Spring, fall, and winter
Access: Trail
Source: Coby Irving Brook
Distance (one way): 250 m/yd
Difficulty: Easy

Elevation: <20 m/yd
Hiking time: 5 minutes
Land ownership: Private
Maps: 21H01-V1
Nearby waterfall(s): Black Hole Brook Fall
Cellphone coverage: Y

Finding the trailhead: Take Highway 221 toward Sheffield Mills and turn north onto Black Hole Brook Road. On top of the North Mountain, continue straight through the intersection with Gospel Woods Road. Drive past the intersection for 5.7 km (3.5 mi) and park just 200 m/yd after navigating a ninety-degree turn. A dirt road here on the right leads toward the Bay of Fundy.

Trailhead: 45°13'53.31"N, 64°29'51.99"W   **Waterfall:** 45°13'57.44"N, 64°29'56.77"W

The hike: This is a short hike to a beautiful waterfall near Baxters Harbour. In an instant, you come up to the rim of a good-size depression considering the size of the brook. The fall is a perched type with a height of probably 12 m (40 ft) framed with sheer rock walls on either side. This fall is a good option to visit if the tide prevents you from seeing the Black Hole Brook Fall. It is easily visited in winter and quite scenic as the layers of water freeze on top of each other to create a giant icicle, which would make an awesome ice climbing location.

The trail is on the same dirt road that leads you to the beach and access to the Black Hole Brook Fall. However, to get to Coby Irving Brook Fall, you need to look for a small path on the west side of the road approximately 250 m/yd after you start.

Bonus fall(s): Drive 3 km (1.9 mi) due east from the parking spot to Baxters Harbour. There is a tall fall that flows into the Bay of Fundy in the small cove north of the Old Baxter Mill Road.

27. Black Hole Brook Fall

200 METRES

Bay of Fundy

Caroline Cove

Dirt Road

Coby

Black Hole Brook

Black Hole Brook Fall

Bigelow Cove Road

Traing Brook

Trailhead

Old Baxter Mill Road

Elevation

60

0

Metres

27. Black Hole Brook Fall

Type: Drop
Height: 12 m (40 ft)
Best season(s): Spring, fall, and winter
Access: Trail, shore walking
Source: Black Hole Brook
Distance (one way): 1 km (0.6 mi)
Difficulty: Moderate

Elevation: 100 m/yd
Hiking time: 1 hour
Land ownership: Private
Maps: 21H01-V1
Nearby waterfall(s): Coby Irving Brook Fall
Cellphone coverage: Y

Finding the trailhead: Take Highway 221 toward Sheffield Mills and turn north onto Black Hole Brook Road. On top of the North Mountain, continue straight through the intersection with Gospel Woods Road. Drive for 5.7 km (3.5 mi) past the intersection with Gospel Woods Road and park just 200 m/yd after navigating a ninety-degree turn. A dirt road here on the right leads toward the Bay of Fundy.

Trailhead: 45°13'53.31" N, 64°29'51.99" W   **Waterfall:** 45°14'2.45" N, 64°29'35.49" W

The hike: On the beach there are some unique geological formations that are fun to navigate. The formations can be covered by rockweed and can be very slippery, but they can make for an interesting way to approach Black Hole Brook Cove, located 250 m/yd to the east. Black Hole Brook has carved a long gorge with steep and tall walls. This cove is entirely filled with water at high tide, so careful examination of a tide chart is necessary before setting off. At the back of the cove, the brook disappears from your view as it does two sharp turns in a row. A 100 m/yd hike on the shoulder of the stream leads to the impressive waterfall hugging the rock face located at the end of the gorge. There is a legend associated with this fall as the burying place of a pirate's treasure that can only be retrieved at the lowest tides of the year. The treasure remains hidden to this day.

From where you parked, walk all the way to the beach and turn to the east. Follow the shoreline all the way to the fall.

Bonus feature: A further 500 m/yd east from Black Hole Brook Cove and Fall lies Caroline Cove, which contains multiple sea caves. There is also a dirt road that ends in Caroline Cove and that can be hiked back to the starting point.

28. Moores Brook Fall

TRUE
N

100 METRES

Elevation
110
50
Metres

Morris Crescent

Prospect Road

○ Trailhead

Moores Brook
Fall ○

101

28. Moores Brook Fall

Type: Fan
Height: 15 m (50 ft)
Best season(s): Spring
Access: River walking
Source: Moores Brook
Distance (one way): 400 m/yd
Difficulty: Moderate

Elevation: <20 m/yd
Hiking time: 10 minutes
Land ownership: Private
Maps: 21H02-Z4
Nearby waterfall(s): Little River Fall
Cellphone coverage: Y

Finding the trailhead: From Highway 101, take Exit 13 onto Highway 12 toward Kentville, and then turn immediately right onto Prospect Road. Drive on this road for about 1.1 km (0.7 mi) until you go over a bridge. Park near the bridge.

Trailhead: 45°3'4.43" N, 64°30'28.11" W   **Waterfall:** 45°3'0.50" N, 64°30'25.89" W

The hike: My history with Moores Brook Fall stretches back to a time where I wasn't such a good waterfall hunter. A walk of more than 45 minutes to the south of the highway left me the nagging feeling that I had chosen the wrong direction as I did not locate a single fall. A short hike to the north of the highway led me to the beautiful Moores Brook Fall in a matter of minutes. This is a good place to stop when you want to stretch your legs for a few minutes on a road trip on Highway 101 to or from the Annapolis Valley. It's a short walk to a massive waterfall of about 15 m (50 ft) located where you wouldn't expect to find anything scenic. There are high cliffs all around the waterfall, which makes this location a little harder to access from an upstream direction. These falls are very impressive any time after a rainfall or during the spring freshet when the water charges down the ravine.

From where you parked, the falls are about 400 m/yd upstream. There is an unofficial trail on the east side of the brook to the fall.

Bonus fall(s): Visit the Elderkin Brook Gorge Trail located in the Agriculture Canada Research Station Site accessible via Highway 1 to see a few more waterfalls.

29. Little River Fall

Type: Drop, cascade
Height: 8 m (25 ft)
Best season(s): Spring and fall
Access: Trail, light bushwhack
Source: Little River
Distance (one way): 1.75 km (1.1 mi)
Difficulty: Moderate

Elevation: 140 m/yd
Hiking time: 1.5 hours
Land ownership: Crown
Maps: 21A16-V1
Nearby waterfall(s): Duncanson Brook Fall, Moores Brook Fall
Cellphone coverage: Y

Finding the trailhead: From Highway 1 west of Wolfville, turn south onto Deep Hollow Road and continue on it across the Gaspereau River for 4.5 km (2.8 mi). Turn right onto Sunken Lake Road, drive 7.3 km (4.5 mi), and park at a dirt road on your right located 150 m/yd past Eye Lane. The trailhead is at the dirt road.

Trailhead: 44°59'23.30"N, 64°27'26.64"W   **Waterfall:** 44°59'26.44"N, 64°28'28.93"W

The hike: In Nova Scotia, there are seldom waterfalls described on the 1:50 000 topographical maps, but Little River Fall is one of them. Do not let the name fool you as the waterfall on the Little River stands at an impressive 8 m (25 ft). Remarkably, the fall is also framed between two huge rock walls that make it more resemble a river in the Cobequid Hills than one located just a few minutes from Wolfville. There is a

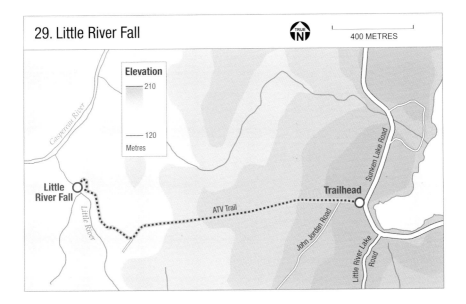

large cleared area at the top of the fall with a sign pinpointing different cities around the world. A gentle path leads down to the base of the fall on the east side of the ravine. At the base of the fall is a deep pool for swimming in the summer months. The fall cascades down the ravine wall and the area exudes a quiet serenity.

From where you parked, walk 100 m/yd on the dirt road to where it divides at a Y intersection. Take the right-hand branch. The old woods road will have a clear-cut on the right-hand side for the first half of the hike. The route largely follows an old woods road turned into an ATV trail before heading through a forest on an unofficial path to the fall. On the ATV trail, you will pass a logged area to the right, a camp on the left, and finally a small bridge over the Little River after walking approximately 1.1 km (0.7 mi). The fall is downstream of the bridge, and there is a faint trail on the east side of the brook. Basically you need to look for the faint trail in an area approximately 200 m/yd before you reach the bridge. A hike of a few minutes through this mixed forest leads to an area that looks as if it's been use for camping and lies just upstream of the ravine and fall.

Bonus fall(s): There are some falls located on the Black River upstream from the power plant known as Three Pools Falls or Hell's Gate Falls. These are located north of Lumsden Dam.

30. Duncanson Brook Fall

Type: Drop, cascade, slider, tiered
Height: 11 m (35 ft)
Best season(s): Spring
Access: Trail
Source: Duncanson Brook
Distance (one way): 1.5 km (0.9 mi)
Difficulty: Easy

Elevation: 120 m/yd
Hiking time: 45 minutes
Land ownership: Nature Preserve
Maps: 21H01-W4
Nearby waterfall(s): Fall Brook Fall (Ettinger Fall), Little River Fall
Cellphone coverage: Y

Finding the trailhead: In Gaspereau, take Greenfield Road up the hill and turn left onto Forest Hill Drive. Park at the end of the road at the entrance to the Nature Preserve. Contact info if necessary: Nova Scotia Nature Trust: (902) 425-5263.

Trailhead: 45°3'12.63"N, 64°19'49.85"W   **Waterfall:** 45°3'33.91"N, 64°19'22.33"W

The hike: Duncanson Brook Fall is a hidden gem located in the 245 ha (605 ac) Wolfville Nature Preserve. I had previously hiked some of the trails in the preserve but had managed to bypass its most significant feature: a series of waterfalls set in an old growth hemlock stand. The largest fall is downstream of the wooden bridge

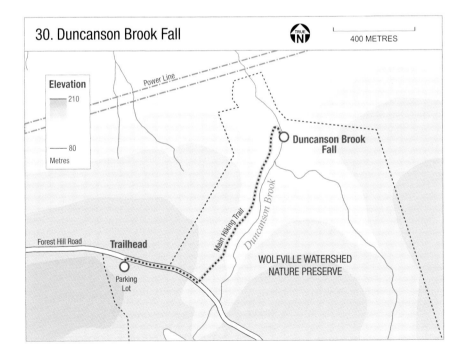

over Duncanson Brook. There are also some remains of a rock wall on either side of the main fall suggesting this might have been the site of a mill of some kind in the past. Upstream from the bridge is an old dam that has sprung some large leaks.

The easiest way to get to these falls is to start on the main hiking trail and turn at the first path on your left. If you miss it, don't worry; you can also access the falls by taking the second path on the left. If you cross Duncanson Brook, you have gone too far. Both paths will be flat at first before plunging into the hemlock ravine.

Bonus fall(s): Continue on Greenfield Road until you come to the intersection with Peck Meadow Road. Continue straight and turn left onto Bishopville Road and park 100 m/yd down. The fall is to your right through the woods.

31. Fall Brook Fall (Ettinger Fall)

Type: Drop
Height: 8 m (25 ft)
Best season(s): Spring and fall
Access: Roadside
Source: Fall Brook
Distance (one way): 1.25 km (0.8 mi)
Difficulty: Easy

Elevation: 40 m/yd
Hiking time: 1 hour
Land ownership: Municipal
Maps: 21A16-Y1
Nearby waterfall(s): Dawson Brook Fall, Duncanson Brook Fall
Cellphone coverage: Y

Finding the trailhead: From Highway 1, turn onto Three Miles Plains Cross Road in Three Miles Plain and drive 800 m/yd. At the stop, turn right onto Windsor Back Road; drive 350 m/yd and then turn left onto a dirt road leading to the Town of Windsor Water Utility Site. Park at the metal gate 250 m/yd after turning onto the dirt road, making sure not to block access to the road.

Trailhead: 44°57'38.85"N, 64°6'45.21"W   **Waterfall:** 44°57'1.46"N, 64°6'26.57"W

The hike: Fall Brook lives up to its name with at least two main waterfalls and many more cascades. The journey to the fall is easy and suitable for just about anyone as the topmost waterfall is accessed via a well-maintained private dirt road. It lies in the protected water supply area for the Town of Windsor. Since the 1800s, the Town of Windsor has used the Mill Lakes as its water supply. There are some step-like 1 m (3 ft) falls upstream before the brook falls 8 m (25 ft) in a true drop. There are some large evergreen trees surrounding the waterfall as well as rocky outcrops, especially on the east side of the brook. The site is visited fairly often and so don't be surprised to see other waterfall enthusiasts. There is another impressive fall further downstream that is taller, but it is not as scenic as it runs over the rock surface.

From the metal gate, walk 1.25 km (0.8 mi) on the dirt road to the topmost waterfall. The main waterfall is just steps away from a large bend of the road and is so close that you will hear the fall before seeing it.

Bonus feature: Continue on Highway 1 all the way to St. Croix. There is a small but scenic dam and spillway on the south side of the highway near Salmon Hole Dam Road.

31. Fall Brook Fall (Ettinger Fall)

TRUE N

400 METRES

Elevation

— 70

— 0

Metres

Windsor Back Road

Dirt Road

Mountain Road

Trailhead

Power Line

Power Line

Lebreau Creek

Fall Brook

O **Fall Brook Fall**

Glooscap Trail

The Glooscap Trail includes a wide area located in the centre and north of Mainland Nova Scotia. The area stretches from Windsor to Truro and includes the Stewiacke Valley. The Glooscap Trail also includes the area west of Highway 311 from Nutby all the way to Cape Chignecto. The main features of this area are the Cobequid Hills that stretch on the north side of Minas Basin. The hills rise from the Minas Basin to a culmination of close to 366 metres (1200 feet) near the Wentworth Valley. Most of the rivers and streams draining the south side of the Cobequid Hills have carved some amazingly deep ravines with a stupendous number of waterfalls to explore. In contrast, I have explored many rivers falling on the north side of the Cobequid Hills between Highway 2 and 104 and have only found significant waterfalls on the Second River and on a tributary of the Roaring River. Although the areas near Truro and Windsor do not offer the same range of elevations, there are some rolling hills that contain many hidden and gorgeous waterfalls. Lastly, although no waterfalls are described for the area around Kennetcook and Noel, there are many smaller falls in this area. There are so many falls located in this region that a waterfall guidebook could be easily written for the Glooscap Trail alone.

42. East River (Five Islands) Fall

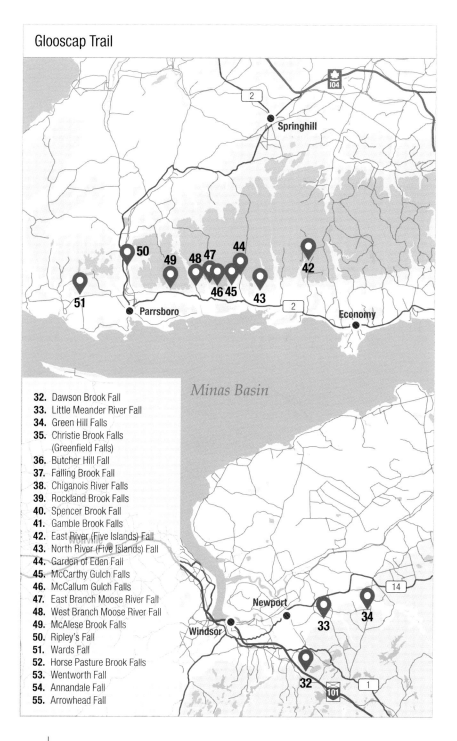

Glooscap Trail

32. Dawson Brook Fall
33. Little Meander River Fall
34. Green Hill Falls
35. Christie Brook Falls
    (Greenfield Falls)
36. Butcher Hill Fall
37. Falling Brook Fall
38. Chiganois River Falls
39. Rockland Brook Falls
40. Spencer Brook Fall
41. Gamble Brook Falls
42. East River (Five Islands) Fall
43. North River (Five Islands) Fall
44. Garden of Eden Fall
45. McCarthy Gulch Falls
46. McCallum Gulch Falls
47. East Branch Moose River Fall
48. West Branch Moose River Fall
49. McAlese Brook Falls
50. Ripley's Fall
51. Wards Fall
52. Horse Pasture Brook Falls
53. Wentworth Fall
54. Annandale Fall
55. Arrowhead Fall

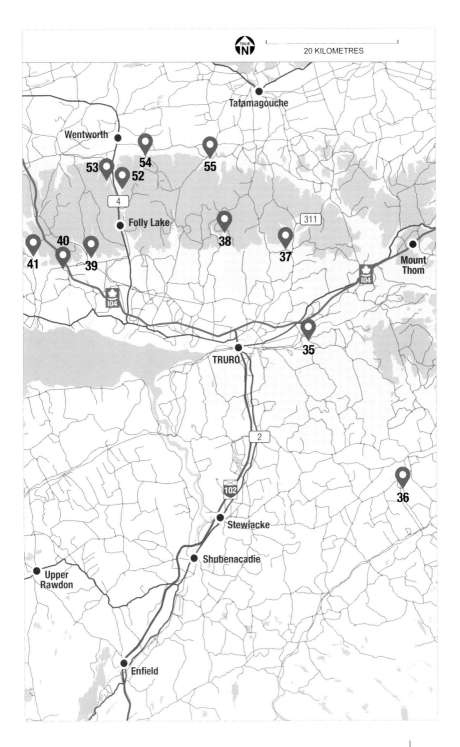

20 KILOMETRES

32. Dawson Brook Fall

TRUE N

200 METRES

Elevation

140

80

Metres

Service Road

101

Trailhead

Woods Road

Dawson Brook

Dawson Brook Fall

32. **Dawson Brook Fall**

Type: Fan
Height: 8 m (25 ft)
Best season(s): Spring, summer, and fall
Access: Trail
Source: Dawson Brook
Distance (one way): 700 m/yd
Difficulty: Easy

Elevation: 30 m/yd
Hiking time: 20 minutes
Land ownership: Private
Maps: 11D13-V2
Nearby waterfall(s): Fall Brook Fall
(Ettinger Fall), Little Meander River Fall
Cellphone coverage: Y

Finding the trailhead: Take Highway 1 between Ellershouse and St. Croix. Turn onto Ellershouse Road and left onto Williams Road. Drive 700 m/yd and turn left onto an unnamed road that parallels Highway 101. Drive 2.4 km (1.5 mi) to a crossroad on the right. Park here. The trailhead is the woods road/crossroad.

Trailhead: 44°55'43.15" N, 63°58'29.41" W   **Waterfall:** 44°55'28.30" N, 63°58'44.57" W

The hike: Dawson Brook Fall is located near Ellershouse, just a few minutes from Highway 101. After walking just a few minutes on a woods road, a trail enters a softwood stand and the sound of the highway quickly dissipates and is replaced by the roar or gurgling (depending on rainfall) of the fall. The fall is located at the top of a small ravine where Dawson Brook first plunges about 8 m (25 ft) hugging the rock surface, followed by two smaller drops of about 0.6-1 m (2-3 ft) each. The area surrounding the fall is dominated by mature evergreens, and the fall is usually well shaded even in the summer months. The path continues all the way to the base of the main fall, but it can be very slippery so use caution.

From your parking spot, follow the woods road perpendicular to Highway 101 for about 350 m/yd. At this point, the logging road splits into two. Take the path on the right-hand side; it enters the woods about 100 m/yd after the split. There should be flagging tape all the way down to the fall to guide the way.

Bonus fall(s): Continue 1.6 km (1 mi) on Ellershouse Road past Williams Road. Turn left onto a gravel road leading to the wind turbines. This gravel road eventually crosses Halls Lake Brook. There is a nice fall where this brook empties into Panuke Lake at 44°54'51.95" N, 64°3'26.32" W.

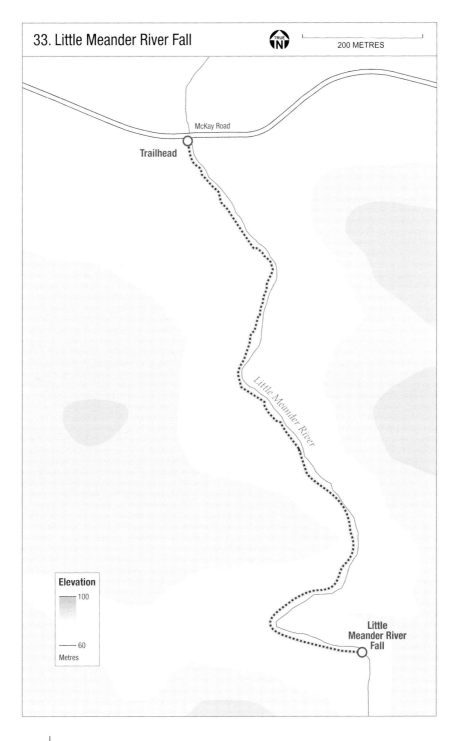

33. Little Meander River Fall

200 METRES

McKay Road

Trailhead

Little Meander River

Elevation

100

60

Metres

Little Meander River Fall

33. Little Meander River Fall

Type: Drop
Height: 6 m (20 ft)
Best season(s): Spring
Access: River walking
Source: Little Meander River
Distance (one way): 1.25 km (0.8 mi)
Difficulty: Easy to moderate

Elevation: 100 m/yd
Hiking time: 45 minutes
Land ownership: Private
Maps: 11D13-V1
Nearby waterfall(s): Green Hill Falls, Dawson Brook Fall
Cellphone coverage: Y

Finding the trailhead: From Highway 101, take the St. Croix exit and turn onto Highway 1 toward Newport Corner. Turn left onto Highway 215 toward Newport/Brooklyn and then right onto McKay Road. Drive about 5.5 km (3.4 mi) until you cross the Little Meander River. Park here.

Trailhead: 45°0'13.84" N, 63°56'32.05" W   **Waterfall:** 44°59'47.63" N, 63°56'17.82" W

The hike: Hidden away on the Little Meander River is a moderate-size fall with a large pool at its base. There are some ATV paths that can lead you to this fall, but it is far more scenic to follow the river from the road to the waterfall. Walking the river is mostly easy as the river is quite broad and largely shallow. There are a few sets of rapids before you reach the main waterfall. There is also an area where there are tall cliffs on either side of the river with some signs of old adits. In times of high water, most of the walking will have to be done in the riparian area alongside the river. There is a large area in front of the fall that is perfectly suitable for a rest, a picnic, or a swim.

To hike to the fall from where you parked, simply head upstream for about 1.25 km (0.8 mi).

Bonus fall(s): Drive 650 m/yd east of Ellershouse Road on Highway 1 and you will cross Weir Brook. Park by the bridge and hike upstream alongside the brook for about 900 m/yd to a small, well-shaded gorge with a waterfall.

33. Little Meander Fall

34. Green Hill Falls

TRUE N

500 METRES

Herbert River

Meek Road

Green Hill Falls

Green Hill River

Small Fall 2

Small Fall 1

Elevation

140

30

Metres

Ashdale Road

Green Hill

Trailhead

South Rawdon Road

34. Green Hill Falls

Type: Fan
Height: 14 m (45 ft)
Best season(s): Spring
Access: Bushwhack and river walking
Source: Unnamed Brook
Distance (one way): 1.2 km (0.75 mi)
Difficulty: Moderate

Elevation: 80 m/yd
Hiking time: 1 hour
Land ownership: Private
Maps: 11E04-W5
Nearby waterfall(s): Little Meander River Fall, Dawson Brook Fall
Cellphone coverage: Y

Finding the trailhead: Take Highway 14 to Centre Rawdon and turn onto South Rawdon Road. Continue until you cross Herbert River and then head uphill to Ashdale Road. Turn right onto Ashdale Road and continue for about 3 km (1.9 mi) down the road. Park near where a brook flows underneath the road (located 600 m/yd before you get to Highway 202).

Trailhead: 45°0'52.88" N, 63°51'29.17" W   **Waterfall:** 45°1'19.50" N, 63°51'36.91" W

The hike: This unassuming small brook near South Rawdon has four distinct waterfalls that plunge their way from a small plateau to the Herbert River. From the trailhead, hike downstream through a mixed forest by walking alongside the brook. The first waterfall is the easiest to access while the last fall on the brook is the tallest. The first waterfall has a large flat and usually dry area in front of it. The other waterfalls have some debris in them but are scenic nonetheless. There are some unofficial trails to follow from time to time and it is easier to stay on top of the ravine for most of the journey except to go to the base of the waterfalls. To access the last and tallest waterfall, it is easier to walk some distance past the fall, descend the hill to the brook, and then walk alongside the brook upstream to the 14 m (45 ft) high waterfall. This last fall has carved itself into the rock walls and remains partially hidden with the canopy of the surrounding evergreen trees.

From where you parked, simply head downstream, following the brook.

Bonus fall(s): The largest fall in this area is seldom visited. After the last fall of the hike, continue following the brook until you reach Herbert River. Follow Herbert River 1.15 km (0.7 mi) downstream (west) to another, unnamed brook. Follow this brook upstream for about 500 m/yd to an 18 m (60 ft) waterfall.

35. Christie Brook Falls (Greenfield Falls)

500 METRES

Salmon River

Christie

Old Union Road

Valleydale Road

Brook

Dirt Road

Trailhead

Old Greenfield Road

Charmac Road

Elevation
— 110

— 30
Metres

Lower Fall

Greg Road

Christie Brook Falls

35. Christie Brook Falls (Greenfield Falls)

Type: Drop
Height: 6, 6, 3 m (20, 20, 10 ft)
Best season(s): Year-round
Access: Trail and light bushwhack or river walking
Source: Christie Brook
Distance (one way): 1.5 km (0.9 mi)

Difficulty: Easy to moderate
Elevation: 80 m/yd
Hiking time: 1.5 hours
Land ownership: Private
Maps: 11E06-Y3
Nearby waterfall(s): Falling Brook Fall
Cellphone coverage: Y

Finding the trailhead: Drive to Valley Station (near Bible Hill and Truro). Turn onto Greenfield Road. Continue for 550 m/yd, then park on a dirt road on your right. It should be straight across from Old Union Road. The trailhead is the dirt road on the right that has large boulders preventing further access to cars.

Trailhead: 45°22'34.53" N, 63°10'59.00" W   **Waterfall:** 45°21'59.29" N, 63°10'47.41" W

The hike: Christie Brook is located in one of J.D. Irving, Limited's designated "Unique Areas" for environmental conservation, and it's also close to Truro. It is sometimes known as Greenfield Falls and contains three distinct waterfalls, each approximately 3-6 m (10-20 ft) high. The path to the falls is well marked to the first waterfall but becomes a bit confusing to reach the upper two. The lowest fall is set in the middle of a large rocky barrier that bisects the whole brook. The upper falls are within sight of each other and have a large rocky outcrop between them. All of these falls seem to have big pools at the bottom, so they are probably good for swimming or running a kayak.

From where you parked, simply follow the trail at the back of the clearing located southwest of the parking area and toward the brook.

Bonus fall(s): Just across from the trailhead, take Old Union Road for 1.4 km (0.9 mi). Old Union Road crosses a brook at this point. There are three small falls downstream on this brook.

36. Butcher Hill Fall

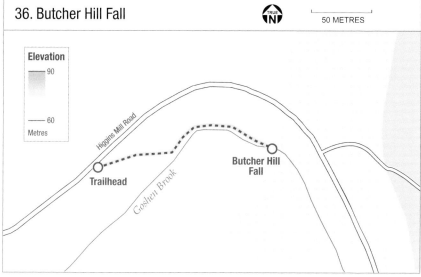

Elevation

— 90

— 60

Metres

Higgins Mill Road

Goshen Brook

Trailhead

Butcher Hill
Fall

TRUE N

50 METRES

36. Butcher Hill Fall

Type: Drop, tiered
Height: 13.5 m (44 ft)
Best season(s): Spring and fall
Access: Trail
Source: Goshen Brook
Distance (one way): 200 m/yd
Difficulty: Easy

Elevation: <20 m/yd
Hiking time: 5 minutes
Land ownership: Private
Maps: 11E03-Z2
Nearby waterfall(s): Gleason Brook Fall, Phantom Fall
Cellphone coverage: Y

Finding the trailhead: On Highway 289 heading northeast, turn right onto Branch Road before you get to Upper Stewiacke. At the end of Branch Road, turn right onto Meadowvale Road. Turn left onto Higgins Mill Road. Cross two bridges that are close to each other and drive 300 m/yd further. There is a parking area on the right with some flagging tape.

Trailhead: 45°10'54.90"N, 63°0'7.67"W   **Waterfall:** 45°10'55.73"N, 63°0'1.90"W

The hike: This is probably the Stewiacke Valley's worst-kept secret spot. The hike is a short one and suitable for all ages. The hike goes through a small softwood mature stand and ends at a gorgeous two-tier waterfall. The upper fall is a true drop of about 9 m (30 ft) framed on either side by tall rock walls. The lowest fall is broad and hugs the rocks as it plunges approximately 4.5 m (15 ft). The lower fall almost prevents you from accessing the upper fall. However, a short but careful hike on the east side of the first fall is all that is required to stand at the foot of the plunging upper fall. Since this waterfall is so close to a road, it is easy to see in all four seasons.

From where you parked, follow the well-worn path from the dirt road to the foot of the fall.

Bonus fall(s): On Meadowvale Road, 1.3 km (0.8 mi) west of Benvie Mountain Road, there is a stream crossing. Findlay Fall is located upstream of here approximately 1.1 km (0.7 mi) in a straight line or longer using the logging roads close by.

TRUE N

400 METRES

Falling Brook

Falling Brook Fall

Upham Road

Power Line

Ash Brook

Elevation

240

90
Metres

Trailhead

Cross Road

37. Falling Brook Fall

Type: Tiered
Height: 15 m (50 ft)
Best season(s): Spring
Access: Trail, bushwhack
Source: Falling Brook
Distance (one way): 3 km (1.9 mi)
Difficulty: Moderate

Elevation: 150 m/yd
Hiking time: 2 hours
Land ownership: Private
Maps: 11E11-X5
Nearby waterfall(s): White Brook Fall, Chiganois River Falls
Cellphone coverage: Y

Finding the trailhead: Take Highway 311 north of Truro and drive to Central North River. Turn left onto Cross Road and drive about 1 km (0.6 mi) to a dirt road on your right. Park here. The trail to the fall is the dirt road.

Trailhead: 45°29'43.42"N, 63°13'30.75"W   **Waterfall:** 45°30'55.00"N, 63°13'44.63"W

The hike: In the Cobequid Hills around Nutby is a beautiful waterfall nestled in the ravine carved by a tributary to the Middle Branch North River. The unique feature of this fall is the pink and black geology of the rocks behind the waterfall. Another remarkable feature of this fall is its location at a point where the tributary joins the main river. The journey to the fall involves mostly a walk on a dirt road, followed by a short bushwhack and a descent to the base of the fall. Close to the edge of the ravine, the forest opens up a bit more and the walking is easier. However, the descent to the base of the fall is quite steep and so caution is advised.

From where you parked, follow the trail and hike about 3 km (1.9 mi), where Falling Brook crosses under the trail. Head downstream for 350 m/yd and you will be on top of the waterfall.

Bonus fall(s): Continue on Highway 311 and turn onto Old Nutby Road. Continue for 2.5 km (1.6 mi) to the intersection of the wind turbine road. Keep left and continue on the old road another 1.3 km (0.8 mi). There is a 6 m (20 ft) fall 500 m/y downstream on the Middle Branch North River.

38. Chiganois River Falls

TRUE N

400 METRES

Trailhead

Upper Belmont Road

North Branch Chiganois River

East Branch Chiganois River

Elevation

— 260

— 130

Metres

Chiganois River Fall

Fall 2

Chiganois

River

West Branch Chiganois River

Fall 3

Fall 4

Fall 5

38. Chiganois River Falls

Type: Drop, tiered, cascade
Height: 15, 9, 8, 6, 5 m (50, 30, 25, 20, 15 ft)
Best season(s): Year-round
Access: Bushwhack and river walking
Source: Chiganois River
Distance (one way): 3 km (1.9 mi)

Difficulty: Moderate
Elevation: 860 m/yd
Hiking time: 3 hours
Land ownership: Private
Maps: 11E11-W5
Nearby waterfall(s): Falling Brook Fall
Cellphone coverage: Y

Finding the trailhead: Starting in Belmont (near Debert), take Belmont Road north to Upper Belmont Road. Turn onto Upper Belmont Road and continue for 10.15 km (6.3 mi). Turn right onto a dirt road at 45°32'49.92" N, 63°20'22.34" W. Drive 1.8 km (1.1 mi) southwest on it. Turn left and follow the dirt road as far as you can. Park anywhere. The dirt road is the trail.

Trailhead: 45°32'4.77" N, 63°20'59.49" W   **Waterfall:** 45°31'30.62" N, 63°20'37.78" W

The hike: The Chiganois River Falls are among the most beautiful falls in Mainland Nova Scotia, but they are somewhat remote. There is a lot of active logging in this area, and new roads seem to appear every year. The directions are to the upstream fall. At the base of the first fall there are a few large boulders and a large tree trunk has been conveniently caught between them to make a bridge to cross the river. It is easiest and best to follow the east side of the river to see the remaining four water-falls as the terrain on the west side is more difficult and dense with trees. The forest around the waterfalls is a mixture of mature hardwood and softwood stands. One of the waterfalls has a large flat area in front of it that is perfect to stop on and admire the fall. Keep hiking close to the river so as not to miss any of the waterfalls. The last fall of the series is located just upstream of an area where the West Branch Chiganois River meets the main river.

From where you have parked the river should be less than 1 km (0.6 mi) away in a southerly direction. Once you arrive at the river, simply head upstream. A GPS would be recommended for this hike.

Bonus fall(s): Sam Higgins Fall is located further downstream on the Chiganois River and can be accessed via a dirt road off Upper Belmont Road.

39. Rockland Brook Falls

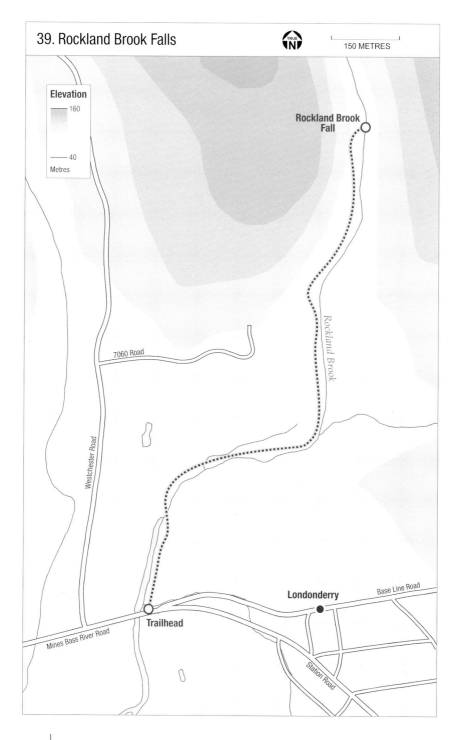

Elevation
160
40
Metres

150 METRES

Rockland Brook Fall

Rockland Brook

7060 Road

Westchester Road

Londonderry

Base Line Road

Trailhead

Mines Bass River Road

Station Road

39. Rockland Brook Falls

Type: Drop, fan
Height: 6, 9, 9 m (20, 30, 30 ft)
Best season(s): Spring and fall
Access: River walking
Source: Rockland Brook
Distance (one way): 1.25 km (0.8 mi)
Difficulty: Moderate

Elevation: 70 m/yd
Hiking time: 45 minutes
Land ownership: Private
Maps: 11E05-Y1
Nearby waterfall(s): Spencer Brook Fall, Gamble Brook Falls
Cellphone coverage: Y

Finding the trailhead: Drive to Londonderry. Locate the Rockland Brook bridge, which can be found on the Mines Bass River Road 100 m/yd east of the intersection with Westchester Road. Park here.

Trailhead: 45°28'34.59" N, 63°36'32.94" W   **Waterfall:** 45°29'7.79" N, 63°36'0.63" W

The hike: A moderate hike near Londonderry is required to see the three 6 m (20 ft) plus waterfalls in a gorge carved by Rockland Brook. At first, the hike is in full view of large deposits of white slag from the old steel and iron industries based out of Londonderry in the late 1880s. The river remains very flat until you reach the waterfalls. The base of the first fall is easily reached by following the shoreline on the west side of the river. For the more adventurous types, the second and third waterfalls can be reached by climbing the natural ledges on the west side of the first waterfall.

The easiest way to the falls is to follow the brook upstream from the bridge on Westchester Road near where you parked. The main falls are located 1.25 km (0.8 mi) upstream.

Bonus fall(s): Continue on Baseline Road from Londonderry toward Highway 4. Salt Brook crosses this road 400 m/yd west of Back Road. Follow this brook upstream for 350 m/yd for a hidden waterfall.

40. Spencer Brook Fall

Type: Drop
Height: 6 m (20 ft)
Best season(s): Spring
Access: Trail
Source: Spencer Brook
Distance (one way): 800 m/yd
Difficulty: Easy

Elevation: 50 m/yd
Hiking time: 10 minutes
Land ownership: Crown
Maps: 11E05-Y1
Nearby waterfall(s): Gamble Brook Fall
Cellphone coverage: Y

Finding the trailhead: In Londonderry, take Mines Bass River Road due west. Cross under Highway 104 and turn right onto Cumberland Road. Continue for about 500 m/yd along this dirt road and park. This road forks ahead. The right-hand side of the fork leads to the river.

Trailhead: 45°28'14.38"N, 63°39'31.72"W   **Waterfall:** 45°28'38.09"N, 63°39'23.95"W

The hike: This is a short walk to a beautiful waterfall located by the Trans-Canada Highway just south of the Cobequid toll plaza. A lot of people drive by this waterfall every day, but probably only a very few of them have seen this fall A dirt road that becomes an ATV path leads you all the way to the waterfall. There is a large pool at the base of the 6 m (20 ft) fall, but it is probably not deep enough to swim. On the east side of the fall is an evergreen-dominated slope all the way to the Trans-Canada Highway. In contrast, the forest on the opposite side is mainly composed of deciduous trees. It is hard to image that the whole valley was devoid of trees by the late 1880s, when there were more than twenty-five iron adits and shafts throughout the upper watershed.

From near where you parked, Cumberland Road forks in two branches. Hike on the right branch as it becomes quickly an ATV-size trail. Walk a few minutes north and you will come by the fall on your right.

Bonus feature: There is an old mining adit on the side of Martin Brook located 1.4 km (0.9 mi) east of Spencer Brook off Mines Bass River Road.

40. Spencer Brook Fall

TRUE N

200 METRES

Cumberland Road

Spencer Brook Fall

104

Spencer Brook

Mines Bass River Road

Trailhead

Great Village Lorneville Road

Elevation

200

110
Metres

41. Gamble Brook Falls

TRUE N

500 METRES

Dirt Road

Trailhead

Blueberry Field

PORTAPIQUE WILDERNESS AREA

Portapique River

Small Falls

Gamble Brook

Gamble Brook Falls

Small Falls

Small Falls

Elevation

260

70
Metres

41. Gamble Brook Falls

Type: Drop, tiered, cascade
Height: 5, 6, 8 m (15, 20, 25 ft)
Best season(s): Spring and fall
Access: Bushwhack and river walking
Source: Gamble Brook
Distance (one way): 2 km (1.25 mi)
Difficulty: Moderate to difficult

Elevation: 140 m/yd
Hiking time: 3 hours
Land ownership: Wilderness area
Maps: 11E05-X1
Nearby waterfall(s): Spencer Brook Fall
Cellphone coverage: N

Finding the trailhead: Take Highway 2 from Glenholme toward Five Islands. Turn right onto East Montrose Road in West Montrose, then left onto Mines Bass River Road. On Mines Bass River Road, turn right onto Old Castlereagh Road. Continue uphill into the Cobequid Hills for 8.5 km (5.3 mi) until a dirt road appears to your right at 45°29'23.1" N, 63°46'11.4" W. Take the dirt road on the right at that location, go around Gamble Lake, and continue to 45°29'37.2" N, 63°44'29.1" W. Park here. A huge blueberry field marks the start of the hike.

Trailhead: 45°29'37.2" N, 63°44'29.1" W   **Waterfall:** 45°29'11.27" N, 63°43'46.41" W

The hike: Gamble (or sometimes named Gammel) Brook is located within the Portapique River Wilderness Area and contains countless waterfalls ranging 5-9 m (15-30 ft). The walk to the first fall is very pleasant with a mature evergreen forest surrounding you. The ground is almost devoid of shrubs, which makes travelling very easy. The main series of waterfalls are impressively stacked on top of each other with at least three different sections that fall over 8 m (25 ft) and a cascade-type fall at the very end. The north side of the brook is best to approach the base of the falls. A GPS is highly recommended for this hike.

The hike starts off in a blueberry field and then enters a dense softwood stand. Gamble Brook is located about 10 minutes due south of the field. From this point the first waterfall is approximately 15 minutes away in a downstream direction. After another 15 minutes the main series of waterfalls is in front of you. After this series of falls, there are a few smaller falls and a narrow section to navigate until you reach the Portapique River.

Bonus fall(s): Once you get to the Portapique River, walk across the river and find a small unnamed brook on the opposite bank located approximately 100 m/yd downstream. Follow it up for 800 m/yd to a beautiful 12 m (40 ft) drop waterfall.

42. East River (Five Islands) Fall

TRUE N

400 METRES

West Branch

Bonus Fall

East River

East River Fall

Dirt Road

Trailhead

Gerrish Valley Road

Elevation

260

160

Metres

42. East River (Five Islands) Fall

Type: Drop
Height: 8 m (25 ft)
Best season(s): Spring
Access: Bushwhack and river walking
Source: East River of Five Islands
Distance (one way): 1.5 km (0.9 mi)
Difficulty: Moderate

Elevation: 140 m/yd
Hiking time: 2 hours
Land ownership: Private
Maps: 11E05-V1
Nearby waterfall(s): North River (Five Islands) Fall
Cellphone coverage: N

Finding the trailhead: In Lower Economy, turn off Highway 2 onto Gerrish Valley Road and drive up the mountain for about 9.5 km (5.9 mi). Park here near a dirt road to the left. This dirt road is the trailhead.

Trailhead: 45°28'29.33" N, 63°58'28.78" W   **Waterfall:** 45°28'29.54" N, 63°59'22.84" W

The hike: This waterfall remains unknown due to its location in the central part of the Cobequid Hills. The first part of the hike, unfortunately, is through a logged area. However, the beautiful waterfall at the end of this hike will make the journey worthwhile. Upon reaching the main branch of the East River, follow the river downstream. Since the area near the river has not been logged, a full canopy engulfs you until you reach the top of the fall. At this point, the descent to the base of the fall can be tricky. The slope on the west side affords more footholds and handholds to get you down safely.

From where you parked, take the dirt road on your left. After 800 m/yd, take a right into the woods for about 400 m/yd until you reach the East River. Head downstream 350 m/yd to a very nice fall.

Bonus fall(s): Downstream of the fall is the confluence of the Western Branch of the East River. Follow it upstream for 200 m/yd to see two other falls.

43. North River (Five Islands) Fall

Type: Drop
Height: 17 m (55 ft)
Best season(s): Spring and fall
Access: Trail
Source: North River
Distance (one way): 1.25 km (0.8 mi)
Difficulty: Moderate

Elevation: 80 m/yd
Hiking time: 1 hour
Land ownership: Private
Maps: 21H08-Z1
Nearby waterfall(s): East River (Five Islands) Fall, Garden of Eden Fall
Cellphone coverage: N

Finding the trailhead: Take Little York Road off Highway 2 in Lower Five Islands and drive for approximately 2.5 km (1.6 mi) until you reach the second of two sharp bends. Park here. The trailhead should be visible to the left.

Trailhead: 45°25'50.75"N, 64° 4'17.63"W   **Waterfall:** 45°26'5.60"N, 64° 4'52.92"W

The hike: This is a well-known waterfall in the Cobequid Hills near Five Islands. The fall plunges 17 m (55 ft) without any contact to the rock behind it. A large flat area in front of this magnificent fall is perfect for relaxing and basking. This is one of the most scenic waterfalls in the Cobequid Hills. Please note, however, that as of 2016 there have been issues with access to the Little York Road. The road is public, but it has been sometimes closed with a metal gate close to Highway 2.

43. North River (Five Islands) Fall

200 METRES

North River Fall

Elevation
190

40
Metres

Little York Road

Old Woods Road

North River

Trailhead

From where you parked, there will be a path leading into the woods on your left. The first part of the hike is on this path, which is an old woods road that has been overgrown by alders. The trail descends a moderate hill, turns to the right, and then crosses a small brook. The brook is very small but has carved out a ravine where the trail fords it. The trail continues uphill and turns to the left toward the river. Once at the top of the ravine, carefully make your way down the slope to the front of the fall.

Bonus fall(s): Drive 5 km (3.1 mi) on Little York Road. At this point, there should be a dirt road on your right. Park there and head into the woods on the left. Walk through the woods to the ravine and drop into it to see three seldom visited waterfalls on the upper reaches of the North River.

44. Garden of Eden Fall

Type: Drop
Height: 20 m (65 ft)
Best season(s): Spring and fall
Access: Bushwhack and trail
Source: West Branch Harrington River
Distance (one way): 1.2 km (0.75 mi)
Difficulty: Difficult

Elevation: 105 m/yd
Hiking time: 2 hours
Land ownership: Private
Maps: 21H08-Y1
Nearby waterfall(s): North River (Five Islands) Fall, McCarthy Gulch Falls
Cellphone coverage: N

Finding the trailhead: From Highway 2 in Lower Five Islands, turn onto Lynn Road and drive 4.5 km (2.8 mi). Park here. The trailhead is on your left.

Trailhead: 45°27'11.67"N, 64°6'45.26"W   **Waterfall:** 45°27'25.8"N, 64°07'12.7"W

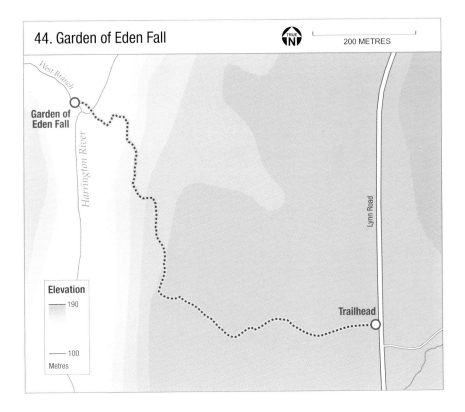

The hike: Garden of Eden Fall is my favourite fall to explore in the Cobequid Hills. This unique waterfall has carved a semicircular canyon and has a true drop of over 20 m (65 ft). There is enough space between the rock wall and the waterfall to make your way behind the veil of water rushing down the cliff. A large pool at the base of the fall completes this picturesque tableau. The hike to this waterfall can be challenging but is worth the effort. Use the GPS waypoint to guide you to the fall. At the back of the clear-cut is a well-established path to Harrington River. Cross the river and you will be at the base of the main waterfall (Garden of Eden Fall).

The first part of the hike is through a logged area and may or may not be flagged. The unofficial path eventually reaches the intact forest that was left on the crest of the ravine of the Harrington River. From this point, the path is parallel to the river for a few hundred metres/yards until reaching a small ephemeral stream that plunges from the top of the ravine to the river below. A path with ropes has been established on the side of this small stream. Take your time and climb all the way down.

Bonus fall(s): From the base of Garden of Eden Fall, go to the right of the fall and scramble up the very steep slope to the top of the fall, then walk 1.5 km (0.9 mi) upstream on this branch of the river to another 11 m (35 ft) waterfall.

44. Garden of Eden Fall

45. McCarthy Gulch Falls

500 METRES

Old Logging Road

Trailhead

Fall 1

Fall 2

McCarthy Brook

Elevation

240

90

Metres

McCarthy Gulch
Falls

45. McCarthy Gulch Falls

Type: Drop, cascade, fan
Height: 6, 11, 6, 8, 8 m (20, 35, 20, 25, 25 ft)
Best season(s): Spring
Access: Bushwhack and river walking
Source: McCarthy Gulch Brook
Distance (one way): 2.5 km (1.6 mi)
Difficulty: Moderate

Elevation: 200 m/yd
Hiking time: 2 hours
Land ownership: Private
Maps: 21H08-Y2
Nearby waterfall(s): McCallum Gulch Falls, East Branch Moose River Fall, West Branch Moose River Fall, Garden of Eden Fall
Cellphone coverage: N

Finding the trailhead: Drive on Highway 2 from Truro toward Parrsboro. Approximately 2.5 km (1.6 mi) past Lynn Road (Harrington River bridge), turn right onto the dirt road at 45°24'55.2" N, 64°08'06.5" W. Drive 3.1 km (1.9 mi) to a Y intersection and keep right. Drive another 1.7 km (1 mi) and turn into the old logging road on your right. Park here.

Trailhead: 45°24'55.8" N, 64°08'7.7" W   **Waterfall:** 45°26'24.8" N, 64°07'55.8" W

The hike: This is a hike through a forgotten gulch located near Five Islands that leads you to five impressive waterfalls. The forest around the brook hasn't been logged for a long time and therefore is surrounded by a mostly mature deciduous forest with patches of evergreens. The terrain near the last three falls is extremely steep and deserves the gulch designation in the topographic maps. A GPS would be advisable to find the brook and falls.

From where you parked, hike the logging road and then enter the mature evergreen forest. Within a few minutes you will reach the brook and the first fall. This is the smallest of the five falls you will encounter on this hike. Turn right to follow the brook downstream 400 m/yd to the next waterfall. This two-tier fall is very impressive with a height of about 17 m (50 ft) in total and a deep pool at its base suitable for swimming. Hiking another 1.4 km (0.9 mi) or so you will bring you to the final three waterfalls of this journey, which are set in a beautiful natural amphitheatre filled with mature hardwoods.

Bonus fall(s): You can visit a smaller fall with a true drop of 8 m (25 ft) located close by on Adams Brook at 45°25'56.1" N, 64°08'02.5" W, just west of the gulch.

46. McCallum Gulch Falls

46. McCallum Gulch Falls

Type: Drop, fan
Height: 12, 9, 6, 8, 5 m (40, 30, 20, 25, 15 ft)
Best season(s): Spring
Access: Bushwhack and river walking
Source: McCallum Gulch Brook
Distance (one way): 2 km (1.25 mi)
Difficulty: Moderate to difficult

Elevation: 200 m/yd
Hiking time: 2 hours
Land ownership: Private
Maps: 21H08-Y2
Nearby waterfall(s): McCarthy Gulch Falls, East Branch Moose River Fall, West Branch Moose River Fall
Cellphone coverage: N

Finding the trailhead: Drive on Highway 2 from Truro toward Parrsboro. About 2.5 km (1.6 mi) past Lynn Road turn right onto a well-maintained dirt road at 45°24'55.2" N, 64°08'06.5" W. Drive 3.1 km (1.9 mi) to a Y intersection and turn left. Continue on the main road for about 900 m/yd and park near where McCallum Brook flows into a small culvert under the road.

Trailhead: 45°24'55.83" N, 64°8'7.77" W   **Waterfall:** 45°26'18.87" N, 64°9'43.36" W

The hike: This is a hike into McCallum Gulch to see five main waterfalls. The first waterfall is 12 m (40 ft) high and is located within about 100 m/yd of the road. The forest is quite dense around this fall but it's worth the effort. As you hike downstream, the forest gradually opens up. After no more than a few of hundred metres/yards, a waterfall of 9 m (30 ft) presents itself. Interestingly in this area of the gulch, the right-hand side of the gulch, which faces north, is composed of evergreen and the soil is covered by moss while the left side, facing south, is an open Acadian-type hardwood forest. There are two more significant waterfalls to observe between this area and where the brook empties into the East Branch Moose River. The hiking is a bit more difficult toward the downstream portion of this brook as the vegetation gets denser and deadfalls are numerous.

At the time I was there, the stream had washed out the road at the culvert making it uncrossable by car. Follow this stream down into the gulch.

Bonus fall(s): Once you reach the East Branch Moose River, walk upstream for 1 km (0.6 mi) and you will come up to a small waterfall framed by rock walls on both sides and a deep pool at its base. Further upstream is the massive East Branch Moose River Fall, which is described next.

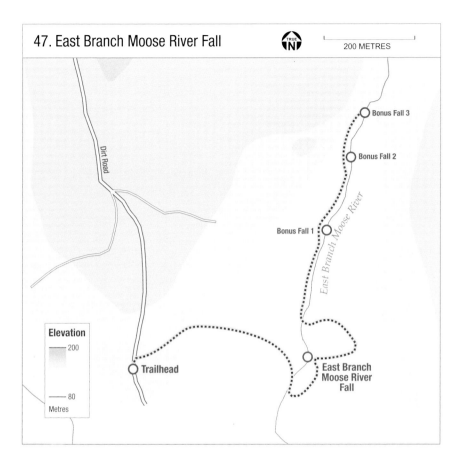

47. East Branch Moose River Fall

200 METRES

Dirt Road

Bonus Fall 3

Bonus Fall 2

East Branch Moose River

Bonus Fall 1

Elevation

200

80

Metres

Trailhead

East Branch Moose River Fall

47. East Branch Moose River Fall

Type: Drop, tiered, cascade, fan
Height: 24 m (80 ft)
Best season(s): Spring and fall
Access: Bushwhack and river walking
Source: East Branch Moose River
Distance (one way): 500 m/yd
Difficulty: Difficult
Elevation: 150 m/yd

Hiking time: 1.5 hours
Land ownership: Private
Maps: 21H08-Y2
Nearby waterfall(s): West Branch Moose River Fall, McCallum Gulch Falls, McCarthy Gulch Falls
Cellphone coverage: N

Finding the trailhead: Take Highway 2 for about 550 m/yd due west of Tidal River Ridge Road to a logging road at 45°25'09.6"N, 64°11'35.2"W. Turn right onto this logging road and drive up the Cobequid Hills for about 4.4 km (2.75 mi) and turn right on a dirt road. Drive 3 km (1.9 mi) and look for some flagging tape on the left leading to the East Branch Moose River Fall. Park here and follow the flagging tape and unofficial path to the fall.

Trailhead: 45°26'31.49"N, 64°10' 53.10"W   **Waterfall:** 45°26'28.00"N, 64°10'36.09"W

The hike: The main fall on the East Branch Moose River is the tallest in mainland Nova Scotia. It is also, hands down, one of the best falls to see in all of Nova Scotia.

From where you parked, walk down the ravine. It is very steep at times, but there are a lot of trees that you can use to slow down your descent. Upon reaching the river, the noise caused by the massive waterfall takes you in the proper direction. The best vantage point is on the east side of the river, so try to find a place to ford. The area around the falls is wide and open and is sometimes subject to heavy misting from the waterfall. On the opposite side of the river, there is a massive rock wall that could be used for climbing depending on the strength of the rock. A climb along the rock wall on the east side of the river in an evergreen forest with a deep moss carpet will lead to a high vantage point overlooking the massive waterfall. There are at least four more waterfalls upstream of the main fall that are worth the effort to visit.

Bonus fall(s): There are three large falls located upstream of the main East Branch Moose River Fall. From the base of the main fall, climb the scree slope on the right (watch out for the poison ivy patch), and follow a faint trail to the top of the main waterfall. From there, there is no dedicated path to see three large and gorgeous falls tucked away in the upper reaches of the East Branch Moose River. As an added bonus, Humming Brook, located to the west of the trailhead, has many smaller but beautiful waterfalls set in a ravine-type setting.

47. East Branch Moose River Fall

48. West Branch Moose River Fall

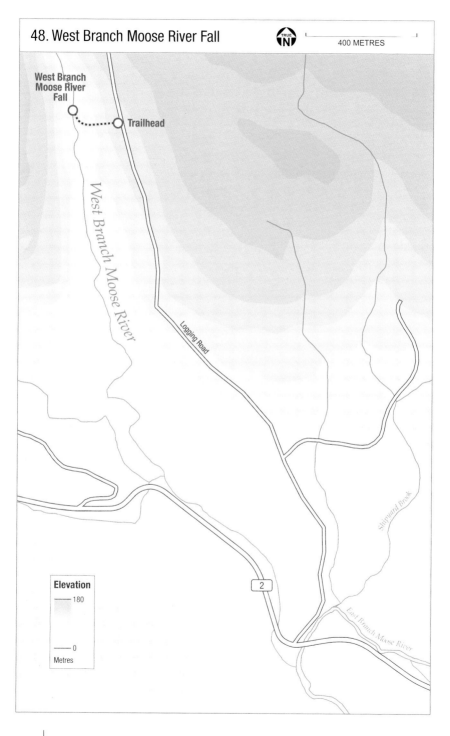

400 METRES

West Branch
Moose River
Fall

Trailhead

West Branch Moose River

Logging Road

2

Shinward Brook

East Branch Moose River

Elevation
— 180

— 0
Metres

48. West Branch Moose River Fall

Type: Drop, tiered
Height: 14 m (45 ft)
Best season(s): Spring and fall
Access: Bushwhack and river walking
Source: West Branch Moose River
Distance (one way): 300 m/yd
Difficulty: Difficult
Elevation: 60 m/yd

Hiking time: 45 minutes
Land ownership: Private
Maps: 21H08-X2
Nearby waterfall(s): East Branch Moose River Fall, McCallum Gulch Falls, McCarthy Gulch Falls
Cellphone coverage: N

Finding the trailhead: Take Highway 2 for about 550 m/yd due west of the intersection with Tidal River Ridge Road to the logging road at 45°25'09.6" N, 64°11'35.2" W. Turn right onto the logging road and drive 2.1 km (1.3 mi). Park here. There should be some flagging tape on the left-hand side of the road leading down into the ravine.

Trailhead: 45°26'8.51" N, 64°12'6.50" W   **Waterfall:** 45°26'9.82" N, 64°12'13.23" W

The hike: The West Branch Moose River contains a massive and fairly well-known waterfall. The hike to the base of the fall takes you through a magnificent softwood stand that has grown on the side of the ravine. Once you reach the river, a short walk on the side of the river is required to stand at the base of the waterfall. Upstream of the fall is the remnant of an old dam, but it's not worth the detour. The waterfall on the West Branch Moose River is smaller than the main fall on the East Branch Moose River but is very impressive nonetheless. A large piece of rock juts out in the middle portion of the fall breaking the drop of water into two different sections at times of low water.

From where you parked, continue down the old logging road. In recent years flagging tape has been put in place to help hikers find the fall, so look for the flagging tape leading you to the waterfall on your left.

Bonus fall(s): Drive 3.8 km (2.4 mi) from Highway 2 to 45°26'56.9" N, 64°11'48.2" W and turn left at the Y intersection. The first fall is off the 90 degree bend (750 m/yd beyond the Y intersection) in an area located at 45°27'06.1" N, 64°12'44.9" W. The second fall is accessed 1.5 km (0.9 mi) further up the same dirt road at a logging road at 45°27'45.4" N, 64°12'37.2" W. The second fall is located at 45°27'40.2" N, 64°13'08.0" W, which is about 800 m/yd from where you will park your car.

48. West Branch Moose River Fall

49. McAlese Brook Falls

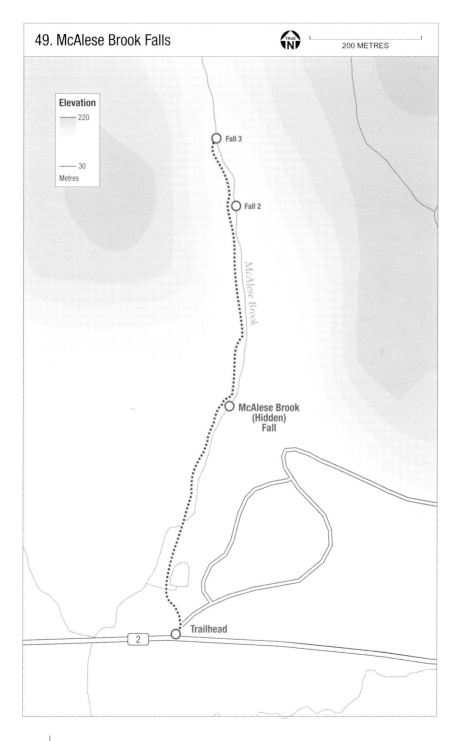

TRUE N

200 METRES

Elevation
—— 220

—— 30
Metres

Fall 3

Fall 2

McAlese Brook

McAlese Brook
(Hidden)
Fall

Trailhead

2

49. McAlese Brook Falls

Type: Drop and tiered
Height: 12, 9, 12 m (40, 30, 40 ft)
Best season(s): Spring and fall
Access: Trail, bushwhack, river walking
Source: McAlese Brook
Distance (one way): 2 km (1.25 mi)
Difficulty: Difficult

Elevation: 300 m/yd
Hiking time: 45 minutes
Land ownership: Private and crown
Maps: 21H08-X2
Nearby waterfall(s): Ripley's Fall
Cellphone coverage: N

Finding the trailhead: Drive on Highway 2 from Five Islands to Parrsboro. McAlese Brook bisects Highway 2 approximately 3.2 km (2 mi) west of Amethyst Drive or 1.3 km (0.8 mi) east of Prospect Road. The pullout area is an old driveway located east of the brook.

Trailhead: 45°25'40.78"N, 64°15'13.91"W   **Waterfall:** 45° 26'09.0"N, 64°15'11.5"W (third fall)

The hike: The Hidden Fall on McAlese Brook has been described in previous guide-books and for a good reason. The Hidden Fall is the terminal fall of a series of four falls located within 100 m/yd in a mature evergreen forest with a high canopy. A long time ago, there used to be a platform to better view the falls.

From where you parked, hike on the trail located on the west side of the brook and ford the brook where required. To reach the foot of the Hidden Fall requires a hike on a well-worn path and on a steep section of the forest and then a careful down climb to the base of the fall. Only by standing at the base will you be able to contemplate this beautiful and hidden waterfall. There is no trail to the two upstream falls shown on the map. To reach the second fall, hike approximately 400 m/yd north of Hidden Fall. The second fall is located at the terminal end of a deep-sided ravine and is hard to reach without ropes. The journey to the third fall bypasses the second fall on its western side with a long climb up the ravine slope. To reach the third fall, descend the ravine slope back to the brook and a short walk of 200 m/yd leads to the final 12 m (40 ft) waterfall. The last fall hugs the rock wall as it loses its elevation and is worth the effort to reach it.

Bonus fall(s): There are falls located on almost all the many branches of Bumpers Brook located east of McAlese Brook.

49. McAlese Brook Falls

50. Ripley's Fall

TRUE N

100 METRES

Elevation

— 80

— 20
Metres

Lakelands

Newville Road

Jeffers Brook

Ripley's
Fall

Trailhead

50. Ripley's Fall

Type: Drop and tiered
Height: 14 m (45 ft)
Best season(s): Spring
Access: Roadside
Source: Jeffers Brook
Distance (one way): 250 m/yd
Difficulty: Easy
Elevation: <20 m/yd

Hiking time: 10 minutes
Land ownership: Private and crown
Maps: 21H08-W1
Nearby waterfall(s): Wards Fall, East Branch Moose River Fall, West Branch Moose River Fall
Cellphone coverage: Y

Finding the trailhead: In Parrsboro, take Beaverdam Road north. Continue on it as it becomes Newville Road. Continue past the intersection with Spence Road for 1.5 km (0.9 mi) to reach Jeffers Brook. Park by the side of the road and head upstream.

Trailhead: 45°27'45.13"N, 64°20'4.30"W **Waterfall:** 45°27'47.25"N, 64°19'49.99"W

The hike: Ripley's Fall is one of the easiest waterfall to see in the Cobequid Hills. Not far north of Parrsboro, Jeffers Brook exits the Cobequid Hills in a 14 m (45 ft) two-tier drop mere steps away from a well-travelled road. A house sits close by on the north side of the river. Although there are no signs restricting access, you should probably ask for permission to visit this waterfall from the owners of the house.

From where you parked on the highway, it is a short walk to the fall. A small unofficial path on the north side of the brook leads all the way to the fall. Just before the waterfall there is a small scree slope that you can scramble up to see the fall from above. Another way to see Ripley's Fall from a lofty position is to hike the forest along the south side of the brook as the brook has carved a tall cliff in front of the fall. A secondary and smaller waterfall lies at the top of the main fall and can be easily seen from the top of the scree slope or from the opposite side of the brook.

Bonus fall(s): If you like bushwhacking, proceed upstream from the main waterfall for approximately 1.5 hours one way to view first a few small falls, then a small rocky gorge, and finally a beautiful multi-tier waterfall.

51. Wards Fall

500 METRES

Yorke Road

Wards Fall

North Branch Diligent River

East Branch Diligent River

Trailhead

Dirt Road

209

Elevation
180

20
Metres

51. Wards Fall

Type: Drop, slide
Height: 6 m (20 ft)
Best season(s): Spring and fall
Access: Trail
Source: Diligent River
Distance (one way): 3.5 km (2.2 mi)
Difficulty: Easy

Elevation: 300 m/yd
Hiking time: 3 hours
Land ownership: Private
Maps: 21H08-V2
Nearby waterfall(s): Ripley's Fall
Cellphone coverage: N

Finding the trailhead: Driving on Highway 2 north from Parrsboro, turn left on Highway 209 toward Port Greville. The trailhead is located off a dirt road located 7.1 km (4.4 mi) after the turnoff from Highway 2 north of Parrsboro. There should be a sign pointing you to the Wards Fall trail.

Trailhead: 45°25'22.68" N, 64°25'28.25" W   **Waterfall:** 45°26'48.53" N, 64°25'11.16" W

The hike: Wards Fall is certainly neither the tallest nor the most beautiful waterfall to be found in this part of the province, but the slot canyons located upstream from it makes this a spectacular place to explore. Although the fall is quite nice, the canyons above are beyond spectacular. The geology in Nova Scotia most often precludes the carving of narrow passages, but they exist in a few places such as this. There used to be a ladder and/or ropes to help you climb above the fall but don't count on those. Climbing to the top of the fall enables you to enter a deep slot-like canyon with a large chamber. The upstream of the canyon has a deep pool that prevents entrance on that side unless you are willing to get wet. Within the slot canyon, the sky is visible but only through a small opening 12 m (40 ft) above your head.

From where you parked, set out on the well-defined trail that leads all the way to the base of the fall, which is located in a mature hardwood forest.

Bonus feature: There are at least three main canyons to see upstream of Wards Fall. Just bushwhack your way upstream past the first fall to explore them all.

52. Horse Pasture Brook Falls

Horse Pasture Brook Falls

Horse Pasture Brook

Hart Lake Brook

Bonus Falls

Wallace Brook

4

Trailhead

200 METRES

TRUE N

Elevation
— 200

— 80
Metres

52. Horse Pasture Brook Falls

Type: Drop, fan
Height: 6, 6, 5 m (20, 20, 15 ft)
Best season(s): Spring
Access: Trail and bushwhack
Source: Horse Pasture Brook
Distance (one way): 2.5 km (1.6 mi)
Difficulty: Easy

Elevation: 120 m/yd
Hiking time: 1 hour
Land ownership: Crown
Maps: 11E12-Z4
Nearby waterfall(s): Wentworth Fall, Annandale Fall
Cellphone coverage: Y

Finding the trailhead: Take Highway 4 from Folly Lake toward Wentworth. As you go down the hill from Folly Lake, take the second road on your right (the first one is gated). The second dirt road is located 1.5 km (0.9 mi) north of Lafarge Lane. Park here. Hike this road 600 m/yd to its conclusion in a cleared area. The path continues toward the fall on the north end of the cleared area and at the foot of the hills located on your right.

Trailhead: 45°34'1.428"N, 63°33'7.48"W   **Waterfall:** 45°34'49.6"N, 63°33'04.5"W

The hike: Most people who visit Wentworth Fall have never visited the beautiful waterfalls located on Horse Pasture Brook on the opposite side of the Wentworth Valley. This is a shame as the hike to the waterfalls is family friendly and very easy as the mature softwood trees are widely spaced and there is very little underbrush. The majority of the hiking is on an old dirt road and would be suitable for cross-country skis or a mountain bike, although a walk in the woods is necessary to reach the falls.

From where you parked, walk along the woods road located at the north end of the clearing and continue as it crosses Hart Brook and then begins to ascend a conifer-dominated hill. The forest then changes to a hardwood dominant stand. Once the road reaches the top of the hill, it crosses Horse Pasture Brook. Turn and follow this brook downstream to see at least seven different falls of all shapes and sizes with the second to last one being the tallest and most scenic fall. The topmost falls are the smallest, and the viewpoints keep getting better and better as you hike down the hill.

Bonus fall(s): The first brook you cross on the way to Horse Pasture Brook is Hart Lake Brook. There is a nice waterfall approximately 100 m/yd upstream from the dirt road. The fall cascades down a nice pink-coloured rock face. There is some deadfall impeding the way to the base of this fall. Hart Lake Brook also contains another massive fall located 200 m/yd downstream from the outlet of Hart Lake.

53. Wentworth Fall

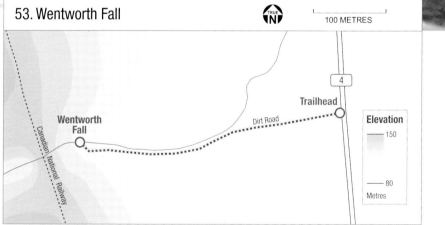

100 METRES

Trailhead

Dirt Road

Wentworth
Fall

Canadian National Railway

4

Elevation

150

80

Metres

53. Wentworth Fall

Type: Fan
Height: 11 m (35 ft)
Best season(s): Spring and fall
Access: Trail
Source: Higgins Brook
Distance (one way): 250 m/yd
Difficulty: Easy

Elevation: <20 m/yd
Hiking time: 10 minutes
Land ownership: Private
Maps: 11E12-Z4
Nearby waterfall(s): Horse Pasture Brook
Falls, Annandale Fall
Cellphone coverage: Y

Finding the trailhead: On Highway 4 south of Wentworth Station, drive to a point 1.1 km (0.7 mi) south of the intersection with Mountain View Lane. Park here. The trailhead is located on the west side of Highway 4 on a dirt road with large boulders preventing vehicle access.

Trailhead: 45°35'17.38" N, 63°33'39.66" W   **Waterfall:** 45°35'16.2" N, 63°33'52.2" W

The hike: Wentworth Fall, located on Higgins Brook, is a fan-type fall that is easily accessible by just about anyone. Depending on water flow, the fall can be heard before it is seen. A large but shallow pool surrounds the base of the fall. Despite many signs of human activity the site is usually quite clean. This is one of those falls that is easily visited even during the winter months. This waterfall is actually constructed. The railroad track located upstream of the fall required the infilling of the natural channel of the brook. The solution was to create a tunnel that passes under the railroad track. The visit to the stream tunnel at the top of the waterfall is difficult but is well worth the detour.

From where you parked on Highway 4, follow the dirt road to the fall. The trail is flat and well established.

Bonus fall(s): There is a series of falls on Dick Meadows Brook located to the south of Higgins Brook on the same side of the Wentworth Valley, almost opposite the quarry location on Folly Lake.

54. Annandale Fall

100 METRES

246

Ax Handle Factory Road

Dirt Road

Blueberry Field

Swan Brook

Trailhead

Elevation
— 170

— 80
Metres

Annandale Fall

54. Annandale Fall

Type: Drop
Height: 14 m (45 ft)
Best season(s): Spring
Access: Trail
Source: Swan Brook
Distance (one way): 200 m/yd
Difficulty: Difficult
Elevation: 25 m/yd

Hiking time: 10 minutes
Land ownership: Private
Maps: 11E11-V3
Nearby waterfall(s): Arrowhead Fall, Wentworth Fall, Horse Pasture Brook Falls
Cellphone coverage: Y

Finding the trailhead: Take Highway 246 at Wentworth Station and drive for about 5.75 km (3.6 mi) until you arrive at 45°37'31.2" N, 63°29'51.1" W. There is a dirt road on the right. Take it past the blueberry field on your left and park at the Y intersection, 700 m/yd from the highway.

Trailhead: 45°37'10.48" N, 63°29'54.25" W   **Waterfall:** 45°37'7.82" N, 63°29'55.95" W

The hike: The tallest fall located near Wentworth Valley is Annandale Falls, and it involves just a quick stroll from the highway to see it. The headwaters of Swan Brook are found very near Debert Lake. Although the hike to the fall is short, the terrain to get down to the base of the falls is very steep. The forest in the area of the fall is composed of tall, mature evergreen trees, and it is quite shaded in the summer. After climbing the ravine, there is no path to the base of the fall. At times of high water, a walk in the stream itself might be necessary in order to stand at the base of the waterfall itself. Depending on water flow in the fall, the area in front of the fall may be exposed to a heavy mist. The east side of the brook, which receives the most mist, is also a straight rock wall down to the brook. Therefore, the west bank of the brook is the best area to view and relax on the side of the fall.

From where you parked, follow the well-worn path into the ravine. There are some ropes in places to assist the descent, but I would be cautious and assess their condition before using them. The falls are up ahead and to your right.

Bonus feature: There is a series of established trails nearby set in a mature hardwood forest. The trailhead is located behind the Wentworth Hostel.

55. Arrowhead Fall

TRUE N

200 METRES

Warwick Mountain Road

Old Debert Road

Byers Brook

Trailhead

Arrowhead Fall

Elevation

180

110

Metres

55. Arrowhead Fall

Type: Drop
Height: 8 m (25 ft)
Best season(s): Spring
Access: Bushwhack and river walking
Source: Byers Brook
Distance (one way): 200 m/yd
Difficulty: Moderate
Elevation: <20 m/yd

Hiking time: 10 minutes
Land ownership: Private
Maps: 11E11-W3
Nearby waterfall(s): Annandale Fall, Wentworth Fall, Horse Pasture Brook Falls
Cellphone coverage: Y

Finding the trailhead: Take Highway 246 toward West New Annan. Turn right onto Warwick Mountain Road and continue past Old Debert Road for 525 m/yd. Park by the bridge over the stream past Old Debert Road.

Trailhead: 45°36'57.72" N, 63°22'22.02" W   **Waterfall:** 45°36'57.56" N, 63°22'19.10" W

The hike: This waterfall comes as a complete surprise when looking at the area close to the trailhead parking. There are some larger hills to the south of the brook, but the waterfall is actually located to the north. The fall is about 8 m (25 ft) high and flows through a narrow ravine. The forest by the side of the road is composed of alders but then becomes dominated by evergreens near the fall. A short walk on the north side of the river is necessary to reach the top of the fall. A careful negotiation of a steep and well-shaded slope is required to get a better view of the waterfall and the deep pool at its base. This pool stays refreshingly cold all summer long.

From where you parked, follow the road to the river and walk downstream to the fall, staying on the north side of the river.

Bonus fall(s): Very close to this waterfall, off Highway 256, is the well-known Drysdale Fall. A visit to this fall can be achieved by following the stream upstream from the bridge.

Sunrise Trail

The Sunrise Trail area includes the region of northeast Nova Scotia from Tatamagouche all the way to Aulds Cove at the entrance to Cape Breton Island. The area includes three significant hill ranges. One is situated in the area between Earltown and New Glasgow and is anchored by the Gully Lake Wilderness Area and Dalhousie Mountain. Although there are a few significant falls in and near the Gully Lake Wilderness Area, the falls become considerably smaller in the Dalhousie Mountain area. The second area is around McLellans Mountain located south of New Glasgow. This area has a few more waterfalls than the ones included in this guide, especially in and around Sutherlands River. The last significant hills are located east of Antigonish in and around the 7,645 ha (18,891 ac) Eigg Mountain-James River Wilderness Area. This third area contains a great many more beautiful waterfalls than could be included in this guide.

65. Cuties Hollow Fall

Sunrise Trail

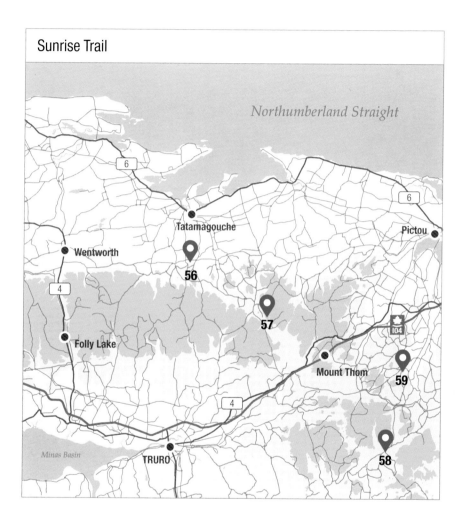

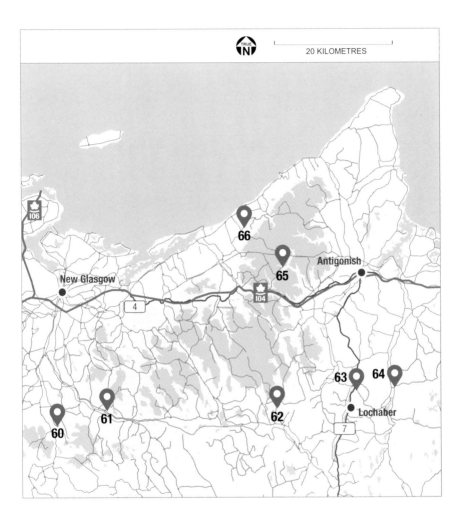

56. Four Mile Brook Falls
57. White Brook Fall
58. Fall Brook Fall (Sheepherders Junction)
59. Gairloch Brook Fall
60. Maple Brook Fall
61. Glencoe Brook Fall

62. Black Brook (East River St. Marys) Fall
63. Hurlbert Brook Fall
64. Polsons Brook Fall
65. Cuties Hollow Fall
66. Vameys Brook Falls

56. Four Mile Brook Falls

200 METRES

Balmoral Road
256
Trailhead

Truro Road

Elevation
100
60
Metres

Four Mile Brook

Lower Fall

Four Mile Brook
Falls

56. Four Mile Brook Falls

Type: Fan
Height: 5, 12 m (15, 40 ft)
Best season(s): Spring and fall
Access: River walking
Source: Four Mile Brook
Distance (one way): 750 m/yd
Difficulty: Moderate

Elevation: 40 m/yd
Hiking time: 1 hour
Land ownership: Private
Maps: 11E11-X3
Nearby waterfall(s): Arrowhead Fall, and White Brook Fall
Cellphone coverage: Y

Finding the trailhead: Drive on Highway 256 (Balmoral Road) between West New Annan and Balmoral Falls. Park approximately 625 m/yd east of the Truro Road intersection where Four Mile Brook flows under Highway 256.

Trailhead: 45°38'17.12" N, 63°16'42.78" W   **Waterfall:** 45°38'6.48" N, 63°16'42.72" W

The hike: There is a series of unexpected waterfalls on Four Mile Brook located on the south side of the Cobequid Hills between the Wentworth Valley and Earltown. The waterfalls can be explored by walking on the edge of the river upstream from the highway crossing. Most of the forest in this area is dominated by mature evergreens, but there are some large maple and beech trees interspersed throughout. The brook is not very wide and fairly shallow. A short and easy walk leads first to a 5 m (15 ft) fall that takes up the whole width of the brook. Between this fall and the next are some areas where rock walls come right down to the edge of the stream and in those areas a climb on the ravines steep slope is required. The second, 15 m (40 ft) fall soon comes into view. This waterfall is very impressive at times of high water as the water rushes out of a small cleft at the top and then spreads in a triangular shape over the whole rock face below.

From where you parked, simply follow the edge of the brook heading upstream.

Bonus fall(s): Head east on Highway 256 to where it ends at Highway 311. Go straight through and continue on Power House Road. Park before the last house and take the path on the left to some amazing geology and falls in the Waugh River Gorge.

57. White Brook Fall

TRUE N

400 METRES

Taylor Road

Taylor Lake

○ **Trailhead**

Elevation

220

140

Metres

GULLY LAKE
WILDERNESS
AREA

White Brook

Kemptown Road

**White Brook
Fall** ○

57. White Brook Fall

Type: Fan
Height: 14 m (45 ft)
Best season(s): Spring and fall
Access: Bushwhack and river walking
Source: White Brook
Distance (one way): 1 km (0.6 mi)
Difficulty: Moderate
Elevation: 40 m/yd

Hiking time: 1 hour
Land ownership: Wilderness area (pending)
Maps: 11E11-Y4
Nearby waterfall(s): Four Mile Brook Falls, Falling Brook Fall
Cellphone coverage: N

Finding the trailhead: Drive to Earltown on Highway 311 from Truro and turn right onto Briorchan Road. Continue up the hill and turn right onto Taylor Road. Taylor Road will fork toward Taylor Lake, keep left at the fork and continue. Park at the end of this road, approximately 3 km (1.9 mi) from its start.

Trailhead: 45°33'24.29"N, 63°6'52.92"W   **Waterfall:** 45°33'8.66"N, 63°6'24.63"W

The hike: White Brook Fall is located a short distance from the 3,816 ha (9,430 ac) Gully Lake Wilderness Area. The large waterfall careens down the rock wall and the round pool at its base is largely devoid of an overhead canopy. The immediate area to the west of the brook and fall is composed of a high rocky cliff while the opposite bank is forested all the way down the slope. There is also a small waterfall upstream of the larger 14 m (45 ft) waterfall.

From the parking area, the hike enters a mature leafy forest that has been selectively logged. The forest is still absolutely amazing with the whole forest floor covered by ferns and a very high canopy. The path ends at the edge of an older logged area. Unfortunately, the brook and fall is on the other side of this area. The struggle through the thick new growth is difficult, but the waterfall is definitely worth it. An easier way to reach the fall is to traverse the new growth area. This new growth area contains some hardwoods, which are easier to traverse than the dense evergreen located closer to the fall. Once you reach the brook, follow it 200 m/yd upstream to the fall.

Bonus fall(s): Continue north on Highway 311 and turn right onto Highway 326 in Earltown. Park at the bridge 350 m/yd away and walk 10 m/yd downstream to MacKays Mill Brook Fall.

58. Fall Brook Fall (Sheepherders Junction)

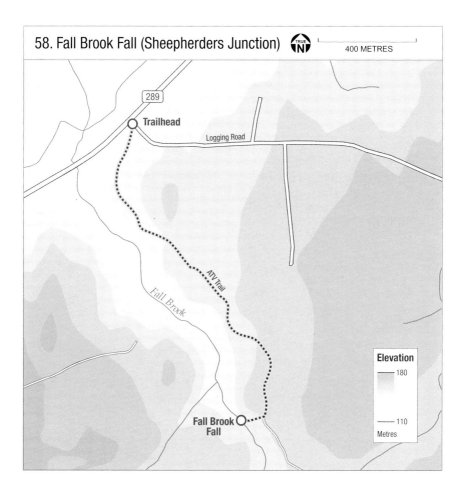

58. Fall Brook Fall (Sheepherders Junction)

Type: Slide
Height: 12 m (40 ft)
Best season(s): Spring and fall
Access: Trail
Source: Fall Brook
Distance (one way): 1.75 km (1.1 mi)
Difficulty: Easy
Elevation: 150 m/yd

Hiking time: 1 hour
Land ownership: Wilderness area and private
Maps: 11E07-W3
Nearby waterfall(s): Gairloch Brook Fall, Maple Brook Fall
Cellphone coverage: Y

Finding the trailhead: Take Highway 289 past Upper Stewiacke and toward Sheepherders Junction. The stream you need to follow is located 1.5 km (0.9 mi) due west of the intersection of Highway 289 and Dryden Lake Road. Park on the side of Highway 289 at the entrance to a logging road.

Trailhead: 45°21'37.78" N, 62°51'4.74" W   **Waterfall:** 45°21'02.7" N, 62°50'44.8" W

The hike: Fall Brook is well deserving of its name. Due to some unique geology in the middle portion of this brook, a massive waterfall has developed. The brook flows in the hills near Kincaid Mountain, and none of the other brooks close by such as Scrub Grass or Suckers Brooks have similar waterfall-conducive geology. The fall is about 12 m (40 ft) high and perhaps 8 m (25 ft) wide and runs on the rock face for the whole drop. In times of low water, a down climb on the side of the fall itself is achievable to get to the base of the fall. The area near the fall is presently pending designation as a wilderness area.

From where you parked, there is an ATV path located on the east side of the river that will take you all the way to the fall. The trail to this waterfall is located within a recently logged area. The trail sometimes disappears because of the logging activity but reappears in the forest ahead.

Bonus fall(s): Not too far away are the easily accessible Burnside Falls. From Highway 289, take Pembroke Road and drive 8.5 km (5.3 mi) to a parking area on your right. Park there and take the stairs to the waterfall below.

58. Fall Brook Fall (Sheepherders Junction)

59. Gairloch Brook Fall

TRUE N

400 METRES

Montreal Road

William Murray Road

Gairloch Brook

Elevation

150

70
Metres

Trailhead

Gairloch Brook Fall

Lairg Road

289

59. Gairloch Brook Fall

Type: Tiered, cascade
Height: 14 m (45 ft)
Best season(s): Spring
Access: Bushwhack and river walking
Source: Gairloch Brook
Distance (one way): 500 m/yd
Difficulty: Easy to moderate
Elevation: 40 m/yd

Hiking time: 45 minutes
Land ownership: Crown
Maps: 1107-W1
Nearby waterfall(s): Fall Brook Fall (Sheepherders Junction), Maple Brook Fall
Cellphone coverage: Y

Finding the trailhead: Take Stewiacke Road (Highway 289) toward New Glasgow and turn left onto Lairg Road. Drive 3.1 km (1.9 mi) and park at St. Andrews Cemetery.

Trailhead: 45°28'42.57"N, 62°49'3.01"W   **Waterfall:** 45°28'41.97"N, 62°48'49.97"W

The hike: A little-known waterfall is located on Gairloch Brook near New Lairg. Travelling down the dusty roads nearby, it is hard to imagine that a large waterfall is hidden in the woods. The waterfall cascades more than drops along the rocky outcrop set in a mixed forest. Depending on water volumes running in the fall, it can be quite easy to climb the brook itself to see the numerous drops. At other times, the forest on the east side is quite open and easy to climb up to reach more vantage points of the waterfall.

The ravine and fall are tucked away behind the cemetery. The descent into the ravine is moderate in difficulty but it is quite short. From there, a short walk upstream in the brook is all that is required to reach this beautiful multi-tier waterfall.

Bonus fall(s): Continue on Montreal Road. Turn left onto George MacKenzie Road and then right onto Millbrook Road. Look for a guardrail on your right 200 m/yd away on Millbrook Road. A significant waterfall is located downslope of this guardrail.

60. Maple Brook Fall

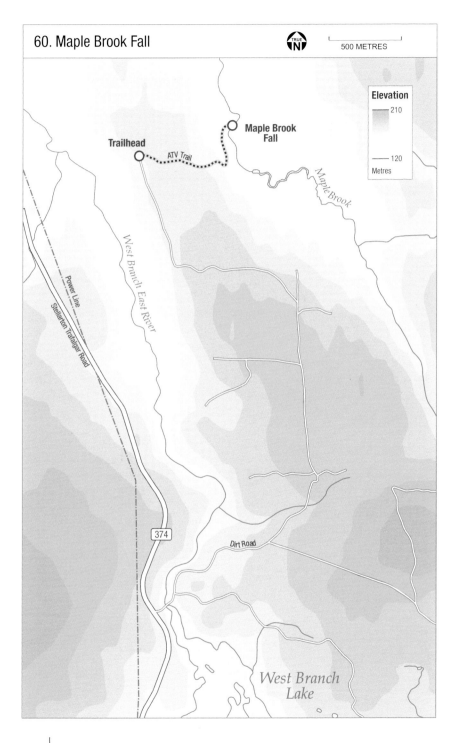

500 METRES

Trailhead

ATV Trail

Maple Brook Fall

Maple Brook

West Branch East River

Power Line

Stellarton Trafalgar Road

374

Dirt Road

West Branch Lake

Elevation
210
120
Metres

60. Maple Brook Fall

Type: Cascade, tiered
Height: 11 m (35 ft)
Best season(s): Spring and fall
Access: Bushwhack and river walking
Source: Maple Brook
Distance (one way): 1 km (0.6 mi)
Difficulty: Easy to moderate
Elevation: 60 m/yd

Hiking time: 1 hour
Land ownership: Private
Maps: 11E07-Y3
Nearby waterfall(s): Fall Brook Fall (Sheepherders Junction), Glencoe Brook Fall, Gairloch Brook Fall, Black Brook (Trafalgar) Fall
Cellphone coverage: Y

Finding the trailhead: Take Highway 347 south of New Glasgow. Drive 7.2 km (4.5 mi) south of Cameron Road in Lorne to a dirt road (as shown on map) on your left at 45°22'05.9" N, 62°39'39.4" W. Turn left onto the dirt road and cross a wooden bridge approximately 200 m/yd later. Turn to the left at the next intersection and again to the left 1 km (0.6 mi) down the road from the highway turnoff. Turn left at the other Y intersection at the 2.8 km (1.7 mi) marker. An ATV trail should appear to your right after approximately 4.5 km (2.8 mi). This is the trailhead. Park here.

Trailhead: 45°23'43.35" N, 62°39'44.48" W   **Waterfall:** 45°23'47.1" N, 62°39'15.2" W

The hike: The fall on Maple Brook remained hidden to me even after numerous explorations in this area. All of these explorations led to some small falls but never quite to the elusive and massive waterfall on Maple Brook near Elgin. The waterfall starts with a broad cascade and loses about 6 m (20 ft) of elevation. It then plunges the last 5 m (15 ft) in a straight drop. The brook has carved a nice mini ravine here, and there are some large exposures of rocks on the east side. The forest around the fall is composed of towering evergreen, and the ground is covered by a deep moss carpet. A fellow explorer shared the location of this fall to me. Many thanks to Graham C.

From where you parked, start down the well-travelled ATV path. Within a few minutes, a short bushwhack of 200 m/yd is necessary to reach the waterfall.

Bonus fall(s): In Hopewell, turn onto Elgin Road and spot the waterfall downstream of the bridge over the West Branch East River.

60. Maple Brook Fall

61. Glencoe Brook Fall

100 METRES

Trailhead

Glencoe Brook
Fall

McLellans
Mountain

McLellan Mountain Glencoe Road

Glencoe Brook

East River East Side Road

Glencoe

348

Elevation

— 140

— 60
Metres

61. Glencoe Brook Fall

Type: Drop, tiered
Height: 15 m (50 ft)
Best season(s): Spring and fall
Access: Roadside
Source: Glencoe Brook
Distance (one way): 250 m/yd
Difficulty: Moderate
Elevation: 40 m/yd

Hiking time: 30 minutes
Land ownership: Private
Maps: 11E07-Z2
Nearby waterfall(s): Chisholm Brook Falls, Maple Brook Fall, Black Brook (East River St. Marys) Fall
Cellphone coverage: N

Finding the trailhead: Take Highway 348 toward Sherbrooke. Turn onto McLellans Mountain Glencoe Road. Drive 450 m/yd and park in the clearing where you can see some ATV trails to your right.

Trailhead: 45°25'7.04" N, 62°33'4.20" W   **Waterfall:** 45°25'5.49" N, 62°32'59.59" W

The hike: The area near Glencoe is known for its many old iron adits but not for waterfalls. The Bridgeville iron mining area, in terms of production, was second only to the Londonderry iron mining sites, with development of the mines in the 1870s (O'Reilly 2004). This is a description of a great but short hike to a large waterfall in an area where you wouldn't expect anything. A 150 m/yd path from the dirt road leads to a viewpoint of the fall. The viewpoint sits on top of a huge scree slope and commands an overview of the two main drops of this waterfall. The descent to the base can be moderately strenuous but not overly difficult. The topmost drop is about 3 m (10 ft) and has a large pool at its base. The pool narrows to about 1 m (3 ft) across. Below the first drop is the second drop of about 8 m (25 ft) with one part of the fall looking like a sluice.

The falls are in a deep gully on the right of the road. You can access them from upstream or downstream by hiking in the brook itself.

Bonus fall(s): If your vehicle has high clearance, you can continue on McLellans Mountain Glencoe Road and turn left onto Brookville Road. Drive on Brookville Road for about 7 km (4.3 mi) to a fall on McLellans Brook on the right.

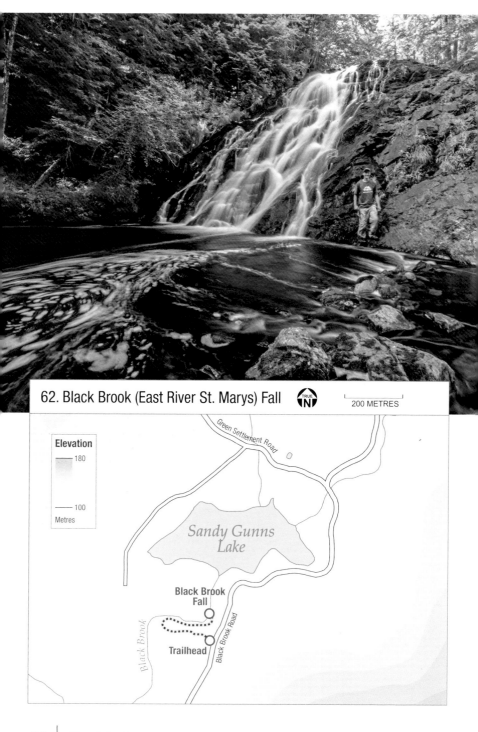

62. Black Brook (East River St. Marys) Fall

TRUE N

200 METRES

Elevation

180

100

Metres

Green Settlement Road

Sandy Gunns Lake

Black Brook Fall

Black Brook

Black Brook Road

Trailhead

62. Black Brook (East River St. Marys) Fall

Type: Fan
Height: 14 m (45 ft)
Best season(s): Spring and fall
Access: Trail
Source: Black Brook
Distance (one way): 200 m/yd
Difficulty: Easy

Elevation: 30 m/yd
Hiking time: 20 minutes
Land ownership: Private
Maps: 11E08-Y2
Nearby waterfall(s): Hurlbert Brook
Cellphone coverage: Y

Finding the trailhead: Take Highway 347 south from New Glasgow. Turn left onto Black Brook Road and drive for about 3.3 km (2 mi) from the intersection. Park here at a small, unofficial pullout area. There is an unofficial path off this road on your left.

Trailhead: 45°25'6.61" N, 62°10'57.26" W   **Waterfall:** 45°25'10.17" N, 62°10'59.28" W

The hike: This is a very easy hike to a beautiful waterfall. This fall is nestled in the hills to the north of Highway 347, which cuts between New Glasgow and Sherbrooke. Above the waterfall is the moderate-size Sandy Gunns Lake. Driving on Black Brook Road toward the lake, the massive waterfall appears quite unexpectedly.

The pullout area where you parked connects to a trail on the west side of the road. The trail leads to a steep descent into a ravine. The roar of the waterfall is quite audible once you reach the side of the brook. A short walk around the base of the hill takes you to a wide and tall fall surrounded by ravine slopes on all sides. The area in front of the fall is devoid of shrubbery due to the foot traffic in this area but has a stand of hardwoods. This area is perfect for a picnic or for relaxing and swimming in the pool at the base of the waterfall.

Bonus fall(s): Continue north on Black Brook Road. Turn left onto Green Settlement Road and continue 2.5 km (1.6 mi) to a bridge over Green Brook. Hike alongside the brook downstream to a small waterfall.

63. Hurlbert Brook Fall

TRUE N

100 METRES

North Lochaber

Lochaber Lake

Elevation

80

30
Metres

7

Middleton Road

Bonus Fall

Hurlburt Brook

Hurlburt Brook Fall

Trailhead

63. Hurlbert Brook Fall

Type: Tiered, drop
Height: 9 m (30 ft)
Best season(s): Spring
Access: Bushwhack
Source: Hurlbert Brook
Distance (one way): 200 m/yd
Difficulty: Moderate
Elevation: <20 m/yd

Hiking time: 20 minutes
Land ownership: Private
Maps: 11E08-Z2
Nearby waterfall(s): Black Brook (East River St. Marys) Fall, Mira Falls (North Brook Falls)
Cellphone coverage: Y

Finding the trailhead: Take Highway 7 from Antigonish toward Sherbrooke. Once in view of Lochaber Lake, look for and turn onto Middleton Road. Go up the hill. When the road starts to level off after 500 m/yd, park your car. The waterfalls are on the south side of Middleton Road.

Trailhead: 45°26'34.98" N, 62°0'41.10" W   **Waterfall:** 45°26'36.66" N, 62°0'51.39" W

The hike: There is a nice series of waterfalls hidden near Lochaber Lake south of Antigonish. Most people drive on this highway between Sherbrooke and Antigonish and never imagine such beauty is hidden opposite Lochaber Lake. There are two main waterfalls on this brook. One is described below and the other one is the bonus falls section. The main waterfall on this brook is over 9 m (30 ft) high with smaller falls above and below.

From the dirt road, a short hike into the mixed forest is all that is required to hear the roar of the falls. There is a bit of deadfall to go over, but it's mainly easy walking until you get close to the brook's edge. Above the main waterfall, there are at least two more 3 m (10 ft) falls, which are easy to reach. However, a descent of some steep terrain is required to get to the bottom of the large fall. Luckily, the terrain is anchored by a few large evergreens and some roots that stick out from the ground.

Bonus fall(s): The tallest fall on this brook (12 m [40 ft]) is actually accessible via Middleton Road, 150 m/yd after the turnoff from Highway 7. You need to go down a steep slope to the base of the fall where you will spot the remains of an old mill. This last fall location was given to me by a fellow waterfall explorer. Thanks to C. Sinclair!

64. Polsons Brook Fall

TRUE N

50 METRES

Upper Springfield Road

Polsons Brook

316

Trailhead

Polsons Brook
Fall

Elevation

80

50

Metres

64. Polsons Brook Fall

Type: Tiered
Height: 5 m (15 ft)
Best season(s): Spring
Access: Trail
Source: Polsons Brook
Distance (one way): 500 m/yd
Difficulty: Easy

Elevation: <20 m/yd
Hiking time: 5 minutes
Land ownership: Private
Maps: 11F05-V2
Nearby waterfall(s): Hurlbert Brook Fall
Cellphone coverage: Y

Finding the trailhead: Take Highway 4 east of Antigonish. Turn onto Highway 316 in Lower South River. Drive 18.5 km (11.5 mi) south on Highway 316 to where Springfield Road intersects the highway. Polsons Brook is just to the south of the intersection. There is a well-defined pullout area by some brush on the south side of the bridge. Park here.

Trailhead: 45°26'49.34"N, 61°55'47.82"W   **Waterfall:** 45°26'47.1"N, 61°55'43.3"W

The hike: The exploration to this waterfall began after I read an excerpt from Fletcher and Faribault (1887), which stated that above the road in McPhee's Mills "a wild and beautiful gorge shows quartz veins white-weathering quartzite and purple slate." The next step was to find the long-lost McPhee's Mills, which does not show up in any modern map. However, an older map of the area near South Lake showed the mill on the outlet of Polsons Brook. I had some doubts as I had driven this road before and never thought a gorge could be located near this area, but they proved to be unfounded.

The unofficial trail starts by the side of the highway near the pullout where you parked beside the unassuming Polsons Brook. A short walk leads to the brook, and from this point on the brook has carved a good-sized ravine from solid rock. The ravine walls and slope can make the hike tricky to the base of the waterfall, which is located 150 m/yd upstream of the entrance of the ravine. The rock walls all along the brook make this a special place to visit.

Bonus feature: Along the south side of the brook and downstream of the fall, there is an old adit that has been driven into the base of a large rock wall.

65. Cuties Hollow Fall

TRUE N

500 METRES

Browns Mountain Road

Trailhead

Cuties Hollow Fall

James River

Elevation

250

100

Metres

EIGG MOUNTAIN - JAMES RIVER
WILDERNESS AREA

Bonus Fall

65. Cuties Hollow Fall

Type: Drop, tiered
Height: 14 m (45 ft)
Best season(s): Spring, summer, and fall
Access: Trail
Source: James River
Distance (one way): 1.75 km (1.1 mi)
Difficulty: Easy

Elevation: 100 m/yd
Hiking time: 2 hours
Land ownership: Wilderness area
Maps: 11E09-Y3
Nearby waterfall(s): Vameys Brook Falls
Cellphone coverage: N

Finding the trailhead: On Highway 104 near Marshy Hope, take Strathglass Road, which becomes Browns Mountain Road. Continue on this road as it climbs and then descends a hill. Park at the old school house at 45°37'30.8" N, 62°09'58.0" W, located on the east side of the road just after you cross a small bridge.

Trailhead: 45°37'28.34" N, 62°9'58.22" W   **Waterfall:** 45°37'33.0" N, 62°09'04.0" W

The hike: This hike is on a well-defined trail into the Eigg Mountain-James River Wilderness Area and ultimately to Cuties Hollow. Fletcher and Faribault (1887) described the falls they found here: "The celebrated falls of James River are best seen from above on the left bank, for from below they can be seen only in part. The water flows in great volume over precipitous rocks, and from a height of about one hundred feet, into a capacious basin, the whole forming a scene of impressive grandeur."

The trail starts to the right (east) of the road. The first 1.1 km (0.7 mi) of this trail has numerous mud puddles to go around before a secondary branch of the James River appears on your left. A 2.5-3.5 m (8-12 ft) stream crossing ford here is necessary to reach Cuties Hollow. After the crossing, another path joins on the left, but the direction to the fall is straight ahead. The trail goes up a small hill and enters a mature deciduous forest. The roar of the waterfall is heard approximately 600 m/yd after crossing the stream. There are numerous paths on your right, some with ropes, to aid you in your 35 m (115 ft) descent to the base of the waterfall.

Bonus fall(s): If you feel like exploring a little more, continue 1.5 km (0.9 mi) downstream from Cuties Hollow. At this point, you should see a tributary on the north side of the river that has a couple of significant falls.

66. Vameys Brook Falls

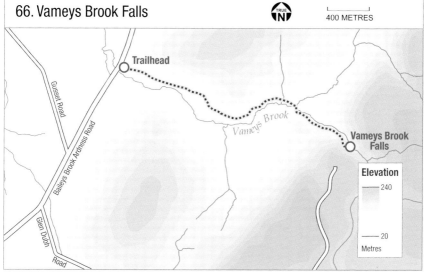

Trailhead

Vameys Brook

Vameys Brook
Falls

Elevation

240

20
Metres

Gusset Road

Baileys Brook Ardness Road

Glen Dubh Road

400 METRES

66. Vameys Brook Falls

Type: Drop
Height: 4, 9 m (13, 30 ft)
Best season(s): Spring and fall
Access: Bushwhack and river walking
Source: Vameys Brook
Distance (one way): 1.75 km (1.1 mi)
Difficulty: Moderate

Elevation: 140 m/yd
Hiking time: 2 hours
Land ownership: Private
Maps: 11E09-X2
Nearby waterfall(s): Cuties Hollow Fall
Cellphone coverage: N

Finding the trailhead: On Highway 104, take Exit 29 and drive north to Baileys Brook. Turn right onto Arbuckle Road, then right again onto Baileys Brook Ardness Road. Continue 1.4 km (0.9 mi) east of Glendu Road to just across the bridge over Vameys Brook. Park here. Follow a dirt road on the side of the brook heading upstream.

Trailhead: 45°41'1.99"N, 62°14'54.14"W   **Waterfall:** 45°40'38.64"N, 62°13'10.60"W

The hike: Vameys Brook Fall is located close to the Eigg Mountain-James River Wilderness Area, and it is my hope that it will be added to this wilderness area in the future. There is no official trail to the two beautiful falls.

From where you parked, follow Vameys Brook upstream or by retracing an old dirt road in the woods parallel to Vameys Brook. After approximately 2 km (1.2 mi) it will be necessary to cross the river to reach the falls located on the tributary found on the south side of the brook. A 500 m/yd walk up the tributary leads you to the first waterfall set amidst of a mature hardwood stand. It is a two-tier fall and is surrounded by steep rock cliffs. Another 200 m/yd upstream takes you past a nice cascade, with the water flowing beside some large boulders. Immediately upstream of the cascade is the last fall. This fall is well worth the hike and again is surrounded by moss and fern-covered cliffs.

Bonus fall(s): There is an enchanting fall located 10 m/yd north of Highway 245 near MacArras Brook. Drive 1.7 km (1.1 mi) east on Highway 245 past Drumglass MacArras Brook Road to find McAdam Brook Fall.

Marine Drive

The Marine Drive stretches all the way from the Halifax Regional Municipality to Canso on the edge of Chedabucto Bay. The majority of significant waterfalls in this region are located well to the north of the ocean shore with the exception of West Sheet Harbour Falls, located downstream of Highway 7 in Sheet Harbour, and the main fall on Liscomb River, which is accessible by a hiking trail. The Musquodoboit River and St. Marys River are the largest rivers in this region and both contain numerous falls, but they are located mainly on their tributaries. Of course there are many more waterfalls in this region than the ones included in this guide, especially those in a line stretching from Sherbrooke to Guysborough.

76. Hartley's Fall

Marine Drive

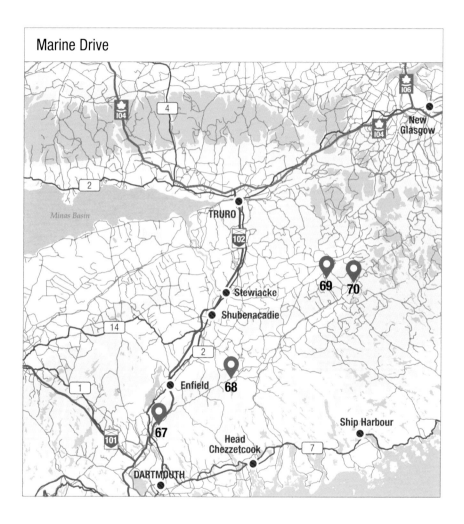

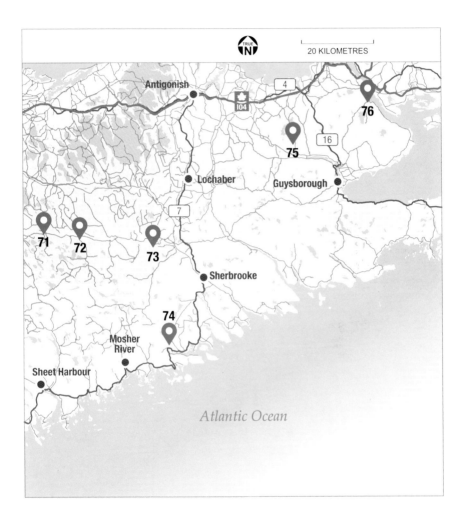

67. Johnson River Falls

400 METRES

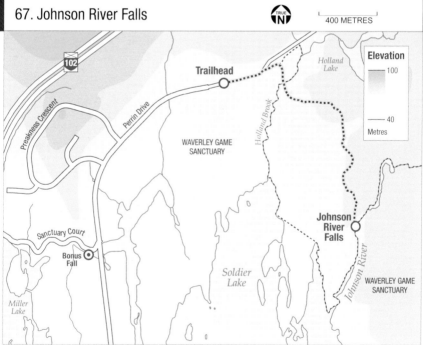

67. Johnson River Falls

Type: Tiered, cascade
Height: 3 m (10 ft)
Best season(s): Spring and fall
Access: Trail and bushwhack
Source: Johnson River
Distance (one way): 2 km (1.25 mi)
Difficulty: Easy

Elevation: <20 m/yd
Hiking time: 1 hour
Land ownership: Private and crown
Maps: 11D13-Z4
Nearby waterfall(s): Nuttal Brook Fall
Cellphone coverage: Y

Finding the trailhead: From Dartmouth take Highway 118 to Exit 14 and turn right onto Perrin Drive. Drive all the way to the end of Perrin Drive and park at a metal gate.

Trailhead: 44°50'13.83"N, 63°34'9.99"W   **Waterfall:** 44°49'39.27"N, 63°33'45.15"W

The hike: The Johnson River Falls are very scenic and are located close to Halifax Regional Municipality. While the headwaters of the Johnson River lie in the Waverley Game Sanctuary, the lower portion and falls do not. Unfortunately there has been a lot of recent logging in the area to the north of the river. The silver lining of the logging is that there is a skidder track to follow within 100 m/yd of the falls. A thin strip of vegetation has been left on the side of the river, but it is enough to shield your view entirely from the logged area once you are looking at the falls. The main falls have two tiers with the lower one having a rocky cleft where the water is funnelled. A visit to these falls in the winter time is not advisable as the snow usually covers all the features.

From where you parked, Perrin Drive continues after the gate as a dirt road. Walk 500 m/yd on the main dirt road to a secondary dirt road on your right. Walk this road another 600 m/yd and turn onto the skidder track on the right. After walking approximately 750 m/yd you veer left off the skidder track to find the Johnson River Falls. A GPS will help you tremendously!

Bonus fall(s): Miller Lake Brook has a fall that is located downstream on the brook flowing under Perrin Drive, 100 m/yd south of the intersection with Sanctuary Court.

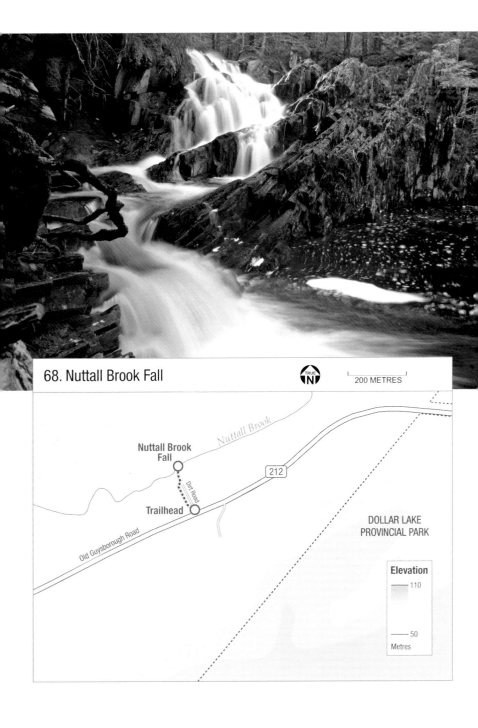

68. Nuttall Brook Fall

TRUE N

200 METRES

Nuttall Brook

Nuttall Brook Fall

212

Dirt Road

Trailhead

Old Guysborough Road

DOLLAR LAKE PROVINCIAL PARK

Elevation

110

50

Metres

68. Nuttall Brook Fall

Type: Drop, tiered
Height: 6 m (20 ft)
Best season(s): Spring and fall
Access: Roadside
Source: Nuttall Brook
Distance (one way): 200 m/yd
Difficulty: Easy

Elevation: <20 m/yd
Hiking time: 10 minutes
Land ownership: Private
Maps: 11D14-W2
Nearby waterfall(s): Johnson River Falls
Cellphone coverage: Y

Finding the trailhead: From the Halifax airport, take Highway 212 toward Dollar Lake Provincial Park. There is a short dirt road on the north side of the highway at 44°56'36.85"N, 63°19'40.32"W. This dirt road is 1.1 km (0.7 mi) before the entrance to the provincial park if you are heading east. Park here.

Trailhead: 44°56'36.85"N, 63°19'40.32"W   **Waterfall:** 44°56'40.89"N, 63°19'48.39"W

The hike: This is a short hike to a nice waterfall located close to HRM. This area, due to its geology and lack of large hills, does not contain many waterfalls. The fall on Nuttall Brook is probably the tallest in the immediate area with water flow on a year-round basis. Close to Dollar Lake Provincial Park, this beautiful 6 m (20 ft) water-fall is well hidden from all human activity but still close to a well-travelled road. A small faint trail leads to the fall as well as a small slate-filled ravine downstream of the fall. The forest is quite typical for this area with a dominance of evergreen and a deep moss cover like a luxurious carpet. The slate rocks on either side of the stream are very slippery after rainfall and incredibly sharp at all times. The location of this waterfall was shared with me by another waterfall enthusiast. Many thanks to Andrew H.

From where you parked, follow the dirt road and enter the woods to the northwest where a faint trail leads to the stream and fall. If you do not spot the faint trail, just head northwest until you cross the brook. Head upstream to the waterfall.

Bonus fall(s): There are a few small falls on Black Brook located in Oldham (near the airport), off the Oldham Mines Road.

69. Gleason Brook Fall

200 METRES

69. Gleason Brook Fall

Type: Tiered
Height: 3, 6 m (10, 20 ft)
Best season(s): Spring and fall
Access: Bushwhack and river walking
Source: Gleason Brook
Distance (one way): 1 km (0.6 mi)
Difficulty: Easy

Elevation: 40 m/yd
Hiking time: 1 hour
Land ownership: Private
Maps: 11E02-V2
Nearby waterfall(s): Phantom Fall, Butcher Hill Fall
Cellphone coverage: Y

Finding the trailhead: Drive to Upper Musquodoboit and continue east on Highway 336. Turn left onto Dean Back Road. Drive 1.4 km (0.9 mi) until you cross over a branch of Gleason Brook, which flows in a culvert under the road. Park here.

Trailhead: 45°10'11.59"N, 62°54'38.91"W   **Waterfall:** 45°10'10.41"N, 62°55'7.48"W

The hike: Not far from Upper Musquodoboit, Gleason Brook crosses Highway 224 before discharging into the Musquodoboit River. From the highway, this stream does not seem to offer much in terms of waterfall formations. However, there are two distinct waterfalls on this brook that are not very far from the road. The first one is only about 3 m (10 ft) while the second one is about 6 m (20 ft) in total, but it is unique as it splits into two drops located close to each other. Unfortunately, reminders of 2003's Hurricane Juan are present on the hike, and the amount of deadfall in and around the brook is a stark reminder of this event. However, the effort will be largely rewarded by the sight of the falls located in a well-shaded ravine.

From where you parked, follow this branch of the brook for 300 m/yd downstream until you meet the main branch. Follow the main branch upstream for about 1 km (0.6 mi) to the fall, which then I would qualify as moderate in difficulty because of the deadfall. Alternatively, you may ask permission of the field owners and cross the fields as the main waterfall is located just upstream of the power lines crossing the fields.

Bonus fall(s): There is a nice ravine with many small falls located close by. Follow Highway 336 east to Lemon Hill Road on your right. Just beside this road is an old logging road. Hike this road for about 1 km (0.6 mi) and head into the woods and down the ravine on the right.

70. Phantom Fall

400 METRES

Elevation

— 130

— 50
Metres

Trailhead

Phantom Fall

336

Dean Back Road

Dirt Road

South Branch Musquodoboit River

Musquodoboit River

70. Phantom Fall

Type: Tiered
Height: 11 m (35 ft)
Best season(s): Spring and fall
Access: Trail
Source: Musquodoboit River
Distance (one way): 300 m/yd
Difficulty: Easy

Elevation: 30 m/yd
Hiking time: 20 minutes
Land ownership: Private
Maps: 11E02-W2
Nearby waterfall(s): Gleason Brook Fall, Butcher Hill Falls
Cellphone coverage: N

Finding the trailhead: Drive to Upper Musquodoboit. From the intersection of Highways 224 and 336, continue 4.5 km (2.8 mi) east on Highway 336 to a dirt road on your right, 200 m/yd after you pass Dean Back Road. Take the dirt road for about 1.8 km (1.1 mi) past a large gypsum outcrop and then over a small bridge. Park approximately at 45°09'33.0" N, 62°53'12.4" W.

Trailhead: 45°9'32.16" N, 62°53'12.13" W   **Waterfall:** 45°9'27.38" N, 62°53'15.78" W

The hike: The origin of the name Phantom Fall derives from a piece of board nailed on a tree by the start of the trail. This is a short, unofficial trail to a large and moderately known waterfall on the upper reaches of the Musquodoboit River. Upstream of the fall is an earthen dam that has created the large lake known as Cox Flowage. Interestingly, the 97 km (60 mi) long Musquodoboit River does not offer any other significant waterfalls on its way to its discharge point into Musquodoboit Harbour. Do not let names such as Blue and Jam Falls fool you as these are mostly large rapids. However, the lack of large features makes this river ideal for canoeing or kayaking neophytes. There are also some smaller falls immediately downstream and further upstream of the main feature. At the top of the fall there is some space to camp, and by the looks of it, this location has been used as such in the past. From where you parked, look for flagging tape or a sign to Phantom Fall on your right. This unofficial trail is flagged and is mostly through an evergreen forest. A steep trail leads to the base of the fall.

Bonus fall(s): There are three main waterfalls on Benvie Brook, which is located west of Upper Musquodoboit. The falls can be accessed by following the brook upstream from Highway 224. The brook crosses Highway 224 by Benvie Hill Road.

71. Black Brook (Trafalgar) Fall

TRUE N

200 METRES

West River St Marys

Cameron Settlement Road

Trailhead

Black Brook

Elevation

140

90

Metres

Black Brook
Fall

71. Black Brook (Trafalgar) Fall

Type: Tiered, drop
Height: 14 m (45 ft)
Best season(s): Spring and fall
Access: Bushwhack
Source: Black Brook
Distance (one way): 750 m/yd
Difficulty: Easy

Elevation: 80 m/yd
Hiking time: 1 hour
Land ownership: Private and crown
Maps: 11E07-Z5
Nearby waterfall(s): Maple Brook Fall,
Chisholm Brook Falls
Cellphone coverage: N

Finding the trailhead: From New Glasgow, drive on Highway 374 south to Trafalgar and turn left onto Cameron Settlement Road. Drive for about 8.7 km (5.4 mi) to where there is a bridge over the Black Brook and a house by the side of the brook. Park here.

Trailhead: 45°17'8.52" N, 62°31'47.16" W   **Waterfall:** 45°16'56.55" N, 62°31'37.09" W

The hike: This is a short hike to a beautifully hidden waterfall on Black Brook located between Trafalgar and Cameron Settlement. The upper reaches of Black Brook sit on crown land, but the area near the bridge is privately owned. Black Brook ultimately flows into the West River St. Marys. The name Black Brook is very popular in Nova Scotia: two other falls described later in this book are located on brooks of the same name. The hike along the stream bank is mainly through mature evergreen trees. At times of low water, a hike in the brook could be undertaken as it is fairly shallow. The fall is beautiful and has a unique feature of a rock wall just in front of it creating a high vantage point to sit down and contemplate this natural beauty.

From where you parked, simply follow the brook upstream to the fall.

Bonus fall(s): If you are making your way down from Highway 374 don't forget to stop in Hopewell (turn onto Elgin Road) to see some waterfalls downstream of the bridge on Elgin Road.

72. Chisholm Brook Falls

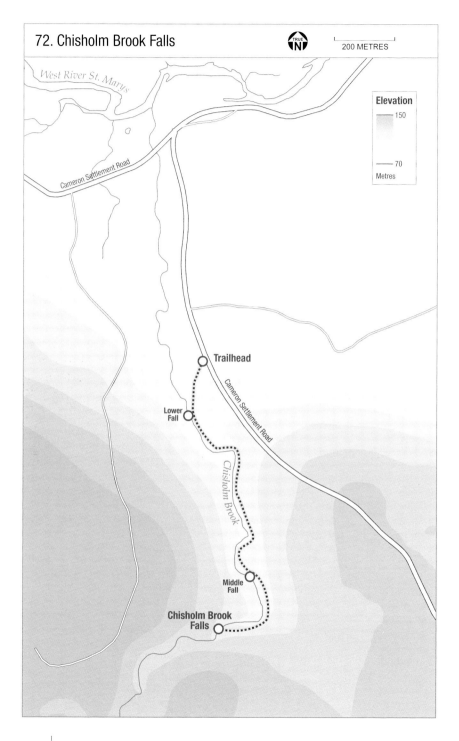

TRUE N

200 METRES

Elevation
150

70
Metres

West River St. Marys

Cameron Settlement Road

Trailhead

Lower Fall

Cameron Settlement Road

Chisholm Brook

Middle Fall

Chisholm Brook Falls

72. Chisholm Brook Falls

Type: Drop and tiered
Height: 3, 11, 11 m (10, 35, 35 ft)
Best season(s): Spring and fall
Access: Bushwhack and river walking
Source: Chisholm Brook
Distance (one way): 1.75 km (1.1 mi)
Difficulty: Moderate
Elevation: 200 m/yd

Hiking time: 2 hours
Land ownership: Private
Maps: 11E08-V5
Nearby waterfall(s): Glencoe Brook Fall, Churn Brook Falls, Black Brook (Trafalgar) Fall
Cellphone coverage: N

Finding the trailhead: Drive on Highway 348 south from New Glasgow all the way to Caledonia. In Caledonia turn onto Cameron Settlement Road on your right, continue for 1 km (0.6 mi), then turn onto a dirt road on your left. Drive about 800 m/yd and park.

Trailhead: 45°16'14.27" N, 62°24'17.69" W   **Waterfall:** 45°15'50.50" N, 62°24'18.40" W

The hike: The modest Chisholm Brook intersects the Cameron Settlement Road near Caledonia before it discharges into the West River St. Marys. However, one cannot fail to notice the mention of waterfalls on this brook in the 1:50 000 topographical maps. It takes a while to drive to the trailhead from almost anywhere, but the many waterfalls on this brook are magnificent, and there are a few more in the area to make this trip worthwhile. The second and third plunging falls feature deep pools for swimming and areas close by to set up a tent.

From where you parked, head west into the woods to reach the brook. A walk of only 150 m/yd through the mixed forest leads you to the first fall. Approximately 500 m/yd and 800 m/yd further along, the second and third plunging falls are nestled in the mature evergreen forest.

Bonus fall(s): Continue on Cameron Settlement Road, heading east, to Highway 374. Approximately 200 m/yd before the intersection with the highway, turn onto a dirt road leading north. Walk on the road heading northeast. Toward the end of the path, you will need to bushwhack to the St. Marys River to a small fall and a beautiful narrowing of the river.

72. Chisholm Brook Falls

73. Churn Brook Falls

1000 METRES

West River St. Marys

ST. MARYS RIVER
CONSERVATION LANDS

**Churn Brook
Falls**

ATV Trail

Trailhead

Cranberry
Lake

West Side River Road

Churn Brook

Elevation

180

50

Metres

73. Churn Brook Falls

Type: Drop, tiered
Height: 6, 8, 6, 11 m (20, 25, 20, 35 ft)
Best season(s): Spring and fall
Access: Trail, bushwhack, and river walking
Source: Churn Brook
Distance (one way): 2.5 km (1.6 mi)
Difficulty: Moderate
Elevation: 150 m/yd

Hiking time: 3 hours
Land ownership: Protected area
Maps: 11E01-Y1
Nearby waterfall(s): Black Brook (East River St. Marys) Fall, Chisholm Brook Falls, Liscomb River Fall, Hurlbert Brook Fall
Cellphone coverage: N

Finding the trailhead: Take Highway 348 to West Side River Road and drive 7.2 km (4.5 mi) to a Y intersection. Continue on the left; the road will do a sharp ninety-degree turn to the north. You will go by a lake on the left and then another intersection about 9.8 km (6.1 mi) further. This time turn right and drive, taking any and all turns that you need to, in order to go the furthest east that you can. Park at a location around 45°14'47.50" N, 62°10'30.27" W. A GPS will prove useful to find the trailhead.

Trailhead: 45°14'47.50" N, 62°10'29.65" W   **Waterfall:** 45°15'5.81" N, 62°9'4.83" W

The hike: This hike will lead you to a series of waterfalls ranging 6-11 m (20-35 ft) on Churn Brook. This brook is located in the St. Marys River Conservation Lands and is protected by the Nova Scotia Nature Trust. The Nature Trust has protected the 90 ha (222 ac) near Smithfield and named it the Hemlock Fall Nature Preserve. The name says it all: the waterfalls are nestled into an old growth hemlock forest. From the eastern end of the logging road all the way to Churn Brook there is actually an old logging road that becomes an ATV trail.

From where you parked, set out on foot on the faint ATV trail heading east all the way to Churn Brook. Once you arrive at the brook, head downstream to the falls.

Bonus fall(s): If you decide to seek the Churn Brook waterfalls from the east side (Glenelg), there are a few falls on the two branches of an unnamed brook located at the intersection of Lead Mine Road and Liscomb River Road. Just follow both branches upstream into the hills rising on the south side of Lead Mine Road.

74. Liscomb River Fall

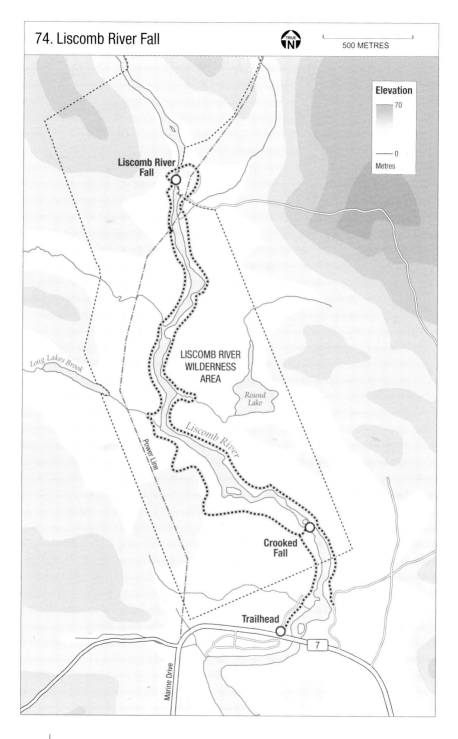

74. Liscomb River Fall

Type: Drop, slide
Height: 9 m (30 ft)
Best season(s): Year-round
Access: Trail
Source: Liscomb River
Distance (one way): 5 km (3.1 mi)
Difficulty: Moderate

Elevation: <20 m/yd
Hiking time: 4 hours
Land ownership: Wilderness area and private
Maps: 11E01-Y5
Nearby waterfall(s): Churn Brook Falls
Cellphone coverage: N

Finding the trailhead: The Liscomb River Trail is located on Highway 7 in Liscomb Mills. There are two trailheads located to the north of Highway 7, one on each side of the Liscomb River. One of the trailheads is located on the Liscomb Lodge Resort property, while the other trailhead is off a dirt road located 200 m/yd east of the bridge. For your safety you can check in at the front desk before and after your hike.

Trailhead: 45°00'46.8"N, 62°05'53.8"W   **Waterfall:** 45°01'57.3"N, 62°06'19.6"W

The hike: The Liscomb River Fall is an absolute gem tucked away on the Eastern Shore of Nova Scotia. The fall is located in the 6,000 ha (14,826 ac) Liscomb River Wilderness Area. The area protects over 40 km (25 mi) of river corridor from the woodland interior to 2 km (1.2 mi) north of Highway 7. This wilderness area is very well known for multi-day canoe excursions. However, a well-maintained 10 km

(6 mi) return trail lets you enjoy its most spectacular sight without paddling: the Liscomb River Fall. The majority of the trail is located beside the river and therefore lets you enjoy the sights and sounds of the river all the way to the fall.

There are two trails that lead to the fall, one on each side of the river. Both trails will have a stream crossing and will contain some slight elevation gains. The west-side trail leads first to Crooked Falls within 600 m/yd after setting off. As the fall finally comes into view, three features stand out. The first is that the fall is situated at the end of a 40 m/yd long rocky canyon. The second is that there is a suspended bridge overlooking the fall and canyon. And the last is that the river branches out above the fall. One side leads to the fall while the other is a fish ladder of 15 pools.

The trail on the west side of the river is as a well-groomed path until the halfway point, where it becomes a wilderness trail with lots of rocks and roots. By contrast, the trail on the east side is a wilderness trail all the way to the fall. Both trails have a stream crossing and bridges may be missing at the time of your hike. In such cases, a detour through the thick forest and a stream fording will be necessary.

Bonus fall(s): Located a few kilometres/miles away on Highway 7 west of Liscomb Mills is Port Dufferin. Park on the dirt road located to the north of the highway on the west side of the river. A 200 m/yd long ATV trail will lead you to a small fall and a swimming hole.

75. Mira Falls (North Brook Falls)

Type: Drop and tiered
Height: 12 m (40 ft)
Best season(s): Spring, summer, and fall
Access: Bushwhack
Source: North Brook
Distance (one way): 1.5 km (0.9 mi)
Difficulty: Moderate
Elevation: 80 m/yd

Hiking time: 1.5 hours
Land ownership: Wilderness area and private
Maps: 11F05-Y1
Nearby waterfall(s): Hartley's Fall, Hurlbert Brook Fall
Cellphone coverage: Y

Finding the trailhead: Take Highway 104 to Lower South River. Turn onto Highway 316 south toward St. Andrews. Turn left onto the Antigonish Guysborough Road and continue until you reach Roman Valley. Turn left onto Afton Road, which becomes North Intervale Road, and continue for 4 km (2.5 mi) until you reach a bridge located at 45°29'17.4" N, 61°39'04.1" W. Park here.

Trailhead: 45°29'16.58" N, 61°39'3.74" W   **Waterfall:** 45°29'19.01" N, 61°39'45.25" W

The hike: The Mira Falls (North Brook Falls) are located in the Tracadie River Wilderness Area. Few other wilderness areas have proportionally as much old growth forest as this one. This inspired me to explore North Brook as well as the description by Fletcher and Faribault (1887) of Mira Falls as an area with "high cliffs overhanging the falls and the gorge below, in which dark grey slates, associated with flinty sandstone and quartzite, have been quarried."

From the bridge near where you parked, follow an old trail for 500 m/yd. Once you reach the end of the trail, the bushwhacking begins. Another 500 m/yd leads to the base of the falls. There are some deep pools and rocks cliffs located at the bottom of the main fall that prevent getting an easy viewpoint from the base. Instead, climb the steep slope on the east side of the brook and then drop back to the stream edge in front of the main waterfall. The path is extremely steep and a rope has been put in place to ease the descent. The last part of the fall is a straight drop of over 12 m (40 ft) with a large and deep pool at its base. There are at least three smaller waterfalls located upstream of the major waterfall and both are separated by deep pools, which are great spots to swim and relax while contemplating the view of the ravine below.

Bonus fall(s): About 1 km (0.6 mi) before you turn onto Afton Road, look for a driveway to your right. The South River flows just to the west of this private driveway. If you follow the river upstream on an old path you will come up to a waterfall on the South River.

75. Mira Falls (North Brook Falls)

TRUE N

|⎯⎯⎯⎯⎯⎯⎯⎯⎯⎯⎯⎯|
400 METRES

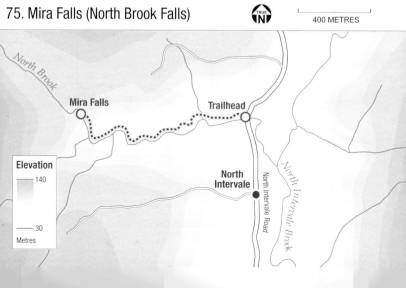

North Brook

Mira Falls ○

Trailhead ○

Elevation

⎯ 140

North Intervale ●

North Intervale Road

North Intervale Brook

⎯ 30
Metres

76. Hartley's Fall

200 METRES

TOWN OF MULGRAVE

Pirate Harbour Road

Trailhead

Hartley's Fall

West Brook

344

St Georges Bay

Pirate Harbour

Pirate Harbour

Marine Drive

Elevation

90

0

Metres

76. Hartley's Fall

Type: Slide
Height: 8 m (25 ft)
Best season(s): Spring
Access: Trail and bushwhack
Source: West Brook
Distance (one way): 100 m/yd
Difficulty: Easy

Elevation: 60 m/yd
Hiking time: 30 minutes
Land ownership: Private
Maps: 11F11-W4
Nearby waterfall(s): Mira Falls (North Brook Falls)
Cellphone coverage: Y

Finding the trailhead: On the Trans-Canada Highway near Aulds Cove, turn right onto Highway 344 toward Mulgrave. Drive for about 1.8 km (1.1 mi), continuing through Mulgrave, and turn right onto Pirate Harbour Road, located before you reach Pirate Harbour. Drive up the hill approximately 1 km (0.6 mi) and listen for the waterfall on your left. Park here.

Trailhead: 45°35'4.30" N, 61°23'34.54" W   **Waterfall:** 45°34'59.49" N, 61°23'36.67" W

The hike: This waterfall is well known locally but sees very little foot traffic. The geology is unique here. The stream has carved out a deep channel and left square rocks on either side of the brook. At the bottom opposite side from where you hiked in is a deep groove in the rock that almost, almost looks like an entrance to a cave. The forest around here is a mixture of hardwoods and softwoods with a couple of mature softwoods by the gorge.

From where you parked, a short hike of 100 m/yd on an ATV-size path from the dirt road takes you down to the bank of the brook. Be advised that the section where the fall is located twists on two ninety-degree turns in about 15 m/yd.

Bonus fall(s): From Highway 344 in Mulgrave, turn onto Mill Street and park. There are a few small falls just upstream of the pond and a park located here.

Marconi and Fleur de Lys Trails

Although this section of the guide is short, this area of Nova Scotia contains a variety of terrain and geology that is mostly conducive to the formation of waterfalls. Often overlooked, but boasting many waterfalls, is the area near Sporting Mountain. One very well-known waterfall, not included in this guide, is situated on the Grand River flowing out of Loch Lomond.

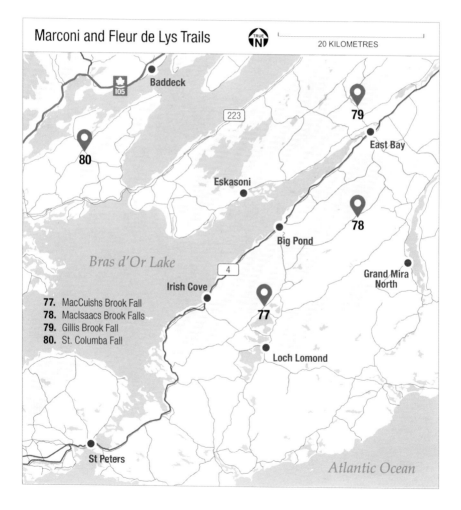

Marconi and Fleur de Lys Trails

20 KILOMETRES

Baddeck

223

East Bay

80

Eskasoni

79

78

Big Pond

Bras d'Or Lake

Grand Mira North

Irish Cove

4

77. MacCuishs Brook Fall
78. MacIsaacs Brook Falls
79. Gillis Brook Fall
80. St. Columba Fall

77

Loch Lomond

St Peters

Atlantic Ocean

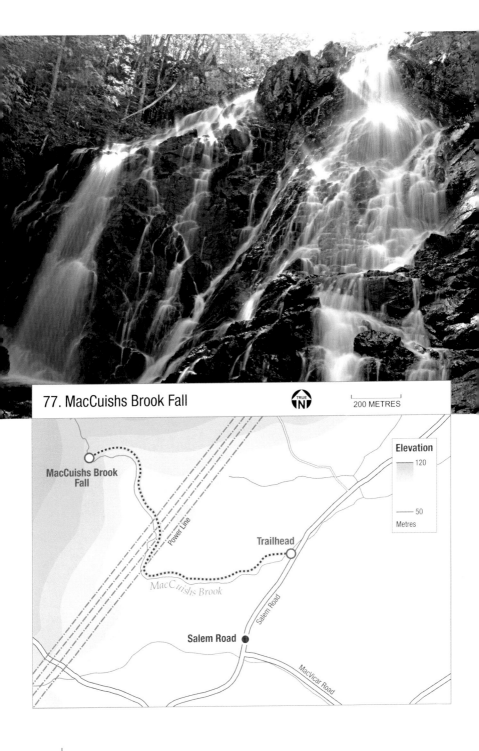

77. MacCuishs Brook Fall

TRUE N

200 METRES

MacCuishs Brook
Fall

Power Line

Trailhead

MacCuishs Brook

Elevation

120

50

Metres

Salem Road

Salem Road

MacVicar Road

77. MacCuishs Brook Fall

Type: Fan
Height: 14 m (45 ft)
Best season(s): Spring
Access: Bushwhack and river walking
Source: MacCuishs Brook
Distance (one way): 1 km (0.6 mi)
Difficulty: Moderate

Elevation: 70 m/yd
Hiking time: 1.5 hours
Land ownership: Private
Maps: 11F15-Z4
Nearby waterfall(s): MacIsaacs Brook Falls
Cellphone coverage: N

Finding the trailhead: From Highway 4 north of Hay Cove, turn onto Hay Cove Road and continue on it for about 15 km (9.3 mi), at which point it becomes Salem Road. Continue on Salem Road until you reach a point about 550 m/yd past the MacVicar Road intersection at 45°48'57.9" N, 60°34'00.4" W. The road crosses the brook with the fall at this location. Park here.

Trailhead: 45°48'57.90" N, 60°34'0.43" W   **Waterfall:** 45°49'9.60" N, 60°34'38.76" W

The hike: This hike takes you to a magnificent waterfall at the end of a small gorge near Loch Lomond on Cape Breton Island. The 1 km (0.6 mi) long MacCuishs Brook rises from the East Bay Hills and is one of the main feeder streams to Lake Uist and ultimately Loch Lomond.

Setting off from the road, hike along the brook until you emerge under some power lines. Continue following the brook upstream toward the fall. The slopes on the side of the brook become steeper and steeper until a point where the best choice is to just follow the stream the whole way. Just before the main fall, there is a huge boulder with ferns on it and some small cascades right beside it. A walk by a sharp bend of the stream is all that is required to stand and contemplate the 14 m (45 ft) waterfall. Many thanks to my fellow explorer and waterfall enthusiast A. Crowley for sharing this fall location.

Bonus fall(s): From Hay Cove Road, turn onto Irish Cove Road and drive almost back to Highway 4. Approximately 200 m/yd after you pass a large quarry on your right you will arrive at a waterfall to your left on Irish Cove Brook.

78 MacIsaacs Brook Falls

TRUE N

200 METRES

MacIsaacs Brook Falls

Power Line

Trailhead

Bonus Fall 1

Glengarry Road

MacIsaacs Brook

Elevation
— 130
— 50
Metres

Mineral Spring Brook

Bonus Fall 2

Gaspereaux River

78. MacIsaacs Brook Falls

Type: Fan
Height: 15 m (50 ft)
Best season(s): Spring and fall
Access: Bushwhack and river walking
Source: MacIsaacs Brook
Distance (one way): 1.2 km (0.75 mi)
Difficulty: Moderate

Elevation: 50 m/yd
Hiking time: 1.5 hours
Land ownership: Crown
Maps: 11F16-V2
Nearby waterfall(s): Gillis Brook Fall, MacCuishs Brook Fall
Cellphone coverage: N

Finding the trailhead: From Highway 4 at Big Pond, turn onto Glengarry Road at Big Pond. Follow Glengarry Road it for about 13 km (8.1 mi) until you arrive at 45°55'20.7" N, 60°23'54.7" W. Park here.

Trailhead: 45°55'17.96" N, 60°23'56.74" W   **Waterfall:** 45°55'23.30" N, 60°24'17.61" W

The hike: MacIsaacs Brook cleaves the East Bay Hills before flowing into the Gaspereaux River and ultimately into the Mira River. The waterfall sits in the middle of the East Bay Hills. The most famous feature of these hills is the ski hill at Ben Eion near Sydney, which is located a mere 6 km (3.7 mi) to the north of the fall.

From where you parked, head directly south to get to the brook. An upstream hike of 700 m/yd along the brook leads to a spectacular 15 m (50 ft) fall over red-coloured rocks in a mature mixed forest.

Bonus fall(s): Walk all the way downstream on MacIsaacs Brook to where it discharges into the Salmon River to view a few more falls.

79. Gillis Brook Fall

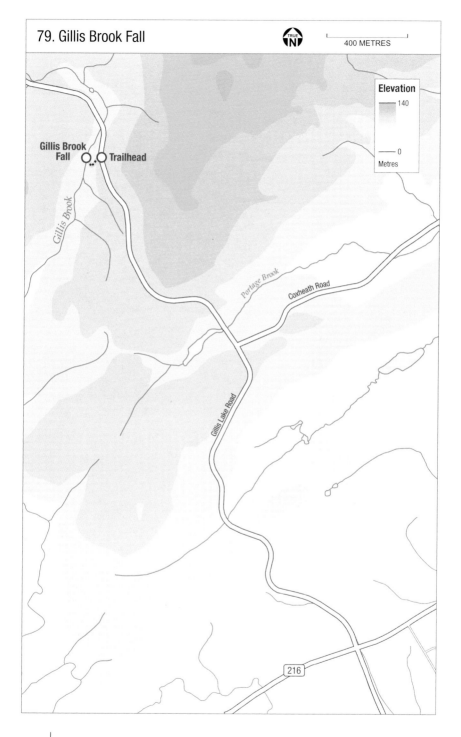

400 METRES

Elevation

140

0
Metres

Gillis Brook Fall   Trailhead

Gillis Brook

Portage Brook

Coxheath Road

Gillis Lake Road

216

79. Gillis Brook Fall

Type: Drop
Height: 6 m (20 ft)
Best season(s): Spring, summer, and fall
Access: Trail
Source: Gillis Brook
Distance (one way): 100 m/yd
Difficulty: Easy

Elevation: <20 m/yd
Hiking time: 5 minutes
Land ownership: Private
Maps: 11K01-W5
Nearby waterfall(s): MacIsaacs Brook Falls, St. Columba Fall
Cellphone coverage: Y

Finding the trailhead: From Highway 4 west of Sydney, turn north onto Gillis Lake Road. Continue 3.3 km (2 mi) until you reach the bridge over Gillis Lake Brook located 1.4 km (0.9 mi) north of the intersection with Coxheath Road. Park downstream of the bridge in the large pullout on the left-hand side of the road.

Trailhead: 46°2'56.87"N, 60°23'32.88"W   **Waterfall:** 46°03'01.5"N, 60°23'33.1"W

The hike: Gillis Brook has its source in the MacDonald Gillis Lakes, which are located in the Coxheath Hills near East Bay. After running its course through some mixed woodlands, it empties into East Bay in Bras d'Or Lake. The beautiful waterfall on this brook is shaded by a mature evergreen forest. This location is not a big secret if you live in Cape Breton, but most other people are not aware of this treasure. There are some ropes to take you down the steep slope to the base of the fall where you can go for a nice dip overlooking the broad waterfall in front of you!

From where you parked, simply follow the trail that leads into the woods and down into the ravine carved by the brook.

Bonus fall(s): On Gillis Lake Road, turn left onto Highway 216 and drive 14 km (8.7 mi) to a bridge over MacIntosh Brook. Follow it upstream to a waterfall.

79. Gillis Brook Fall

TRUE N

200 METRES

Washabuck River

Washabuck Road

St. Columba Road

Trailhead

St. Columba Fall

Elevation

100

0

Metres

CAINS MOUNTAIN
WILDERNESS
AREA

Highland Hill Road

80. St. Columba Fall

Type: Drop
Height: 9 m (30 ft)
Best season(s): Spring and fall
Access: Roadside
Source: Washabuck Tributary Brook
Distance (one way): 100 m/yd
Difficulty: Easy

Elevation: <20 m/yd
Hiking time: 5 minutes
Land ownership: Wilderness area
Maps: 11F15-W1
Nearby waterfall(s): Myles Doyle Fall, Gillis Brook Fall
Cellphone coverage: Y

Finding the trailhead: In Little Narrows, take Little Narrows Road to St. Columba Road. At the intersection continue straight on St. Columba Road for 850 m/yd and up a hill. Park here.

Trailhead: 46°0'30.38"N, 60°52'38.49"W   **Waterfall:** 46°0'6.73"N, 60°52'33.27"W

The hike: The St. Columba Fall sits in the Cains Mountain Wilderness Area. This wilderness area protects some mature hardwood and rare karst forest near Iona. This is a really short hike, suitable for anybody, leading to a magnificent waterfall. The waterfall leaves the rock face for about 6 m (20 ft) and then cascades down the rest of the way to a moderately deep pool. There is a secondary, smaller fall located downstream. The forest around the falls is mostly mature conifers with a few hardwoods. The upper fall is deeply shaded, and the rock formation offers a lot of nooks and crannies, although they are too small for any human to crawl through.

From where you parked, you will see a small trail to your right at a ninety-degree left turn. Follow it to the fall.

Bonus feature: Drive all the way east on the St. Columba Road and then turn right on Gillis Point Road. Drive 2 km (1.25 mi) south to Plaster Cove and its iconic gypsum outcrops on the side of Bras d'Or Lake.

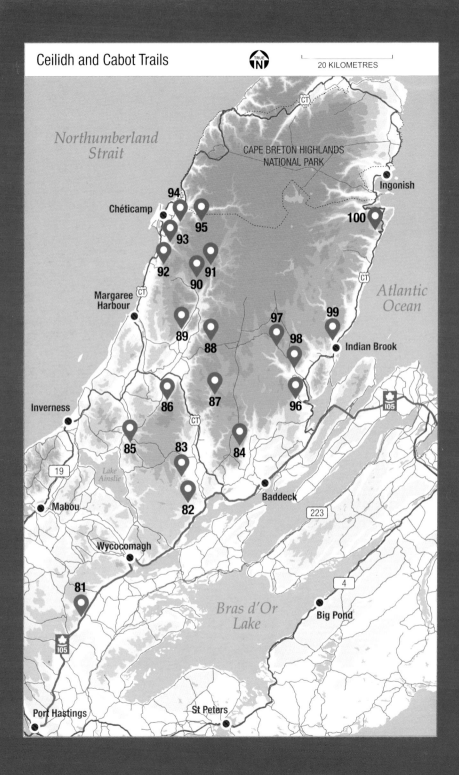

Ceilidh and Cabot Trails

20 KILOMETRES

Northumberland
Strait

CAPE BRETON HIGHLANDS
NATIONAL PARK

Ingonish

Chéticamp

94

95

93

92

Margaree
Harbour

91

90

Atlantic
Ocean

100

89

88

97

99

98

Indian Brook

Inverness

86

87

96

85

83

84

19

Lake
Ainslie

82

Baddeck

223

Mabou

Wycocomagh

81

Bras d'Or
Lake

Big Pond

4

105

Port Hastings

St Peters

Ceilidh and Cabot Trails

This area of Cape Breton could easily have a guide to more than four hundred significant waterfalls, as the majority of the area is dominated by large hills. From the Creignish Hills to the south, the Mabou Highlands to the west, and the Highlands to the north, most of the hills are cleaved by brooks and rivers that form an astounding number of waterfalls. Some of these falls can be very easy to reach while others will only be visited by hard-core explorers or viewed via satellite imagery. Every trip I take to this part of Cape Breton results not only in more falls viewed but also an increase in potential areas to visit next time. This area of Cape Breton contains the Cape Breton Highlands National Park. The park offers many waterfall hikes that are not included in this guide as the information is readily available from other sources. Over the years, I have also explored a few significant waterfalls in the park that do not have any trails leading to them such as Rigwash, Aucoin, and South Branch Corney Brook Falls, to name just a few. The waterfall in the Uisge Ban Fall Provincial Park near Baddeck is easy to find and therefore not included in this guide, but should be high on your list of waterfalls to visit in Nova Scotia. There are also a lot of waterfalls in the hills on both sides of the Aspy River. The falls on Archies Brook and Grey Hollow Brook are somewhat known. There are also many waterfalls on the Blair River system, which leads to Pollets Cove, as well as on the Red River flowing toward Pleasant Bay. Unfortunately, these waterfalls are not included in this guide as I did not bring a camera on these trips when I made them a decade or so ago.

81. Myles Doyle Fall
82. Second Branch Humes River Fall
83. Black Brook (Middle River) Fall
84. MacRae Brook Falls
85. Egypt Fall
86. Tompkins Brook Fall
87. Bothan Brook Fall
88. Martha Brook Fall
89. Lavis Brook Falls
90. Turner Brook Fall
91. Rocky Brook Fall
92. Factory Brook Fall
93. Farm Brook Fall
94. Fiset Brook Fall
95. Faribault Brook Fall
96. Goose Cove Brook Falls
97. North River Fall
98. Timber Brook Fall
99. Great Falls
100. Pathend Brook Falls

81. Myles Doyle Fall

200 METRES

Elevation
160

20
Metres

Melford

Glen Brook

River Denys Road

105

Myles Doyle
Fall

Trailhead

81. Myles Doyle Fall

Type: Tiered
Height: 12 m (40 ft)
Best season(s): Spring and fall
Access: Roadside
Source: Glen Brook
Distance (one way): 100 m/yd
Difficulty: Easy

Elevation: <20 m/yd
Hiking time: 2 minutes
Land ownership: Crown
Maps: 11F14-X3
Nearby waterfall(s): St. Columba Fall
Cellphone coverage: Y

Finding the trailhead: From the Trans-Canada Highway south of Melford, turn onto River Denys Road. Continue for 2 km (1.25 mi) up a 100 m/yd ascent to the fall located by the right side of this road. Park here.

Trailhead: 45°52'11.26"N, 61°15'41.84"W   **Waterfall:** 45°52'0.24"N, 61°16'50.53"W

The hike: Not far from the Trans-Canada Highway in Cape Breton Island lies a beautiful waterfall actively carving sinuous passages through hard rocks in the Creignish Hills. There is a long history of humans at this site including the establishment of a tannery. The lovely Myles Doyle Fall is easily accessible and even more agreeable with the recent addition of a staircase as well as the installation of a bench and picnic table. The forest in this area is beautiful as you drive up River Denys Road from the highway. In winter it would be a great cross-country journey with all the uphill on the front end of the trip and a nice glide back down at the end.

From where you parked, simply walk to the fall.

Bonus fall(s): Drive 2.6 km (1.6 mi) on Old Mill Road, located just northeast of River Denys Road. Park at a culvert and follow a branch of Glen Brook upstream to a narrowing gorge and numerous small waterfalls with the topmost being the tallest at approximately 6 m (20 ft).

82. Second Branch Humes River Fall

Type: Drop
Height: 15 m (50 ft)
Best season(s): Spring, summer, and fall
Access: Trail, bushwhack
Source: Second Branch Humes River
Distance (one way): 5 km (3.1 mi)
Difficulty: Moderate to difficult

Elevation: 300 m/yd
Hiking time: 3 hours
Land ownership: Wilderness area
Maps: 11K02-V4
Nearby waterfall(s): Black Brook (Middle River) Fall, St. Columba Fall
Cellphone coverage: Y

Finding the trailhead: On Highway 105 from Whycocomagh toward Nyanza, drive to the Humes Rear Road, located 1 km (0.6 mi) southwest of the bridge over Middle River. Drive on the Humes Rear Road for 1.2 km (0.75 mi) and park near the school and baseball field. The road continues from this parking spot but it becomes an ATV/snowmobile trail.

Trailhead: 46°04'22.52" N, 60°55'26.42" W   **Waterfall:** 46°03'49.5" N, 60°58'35.8" W

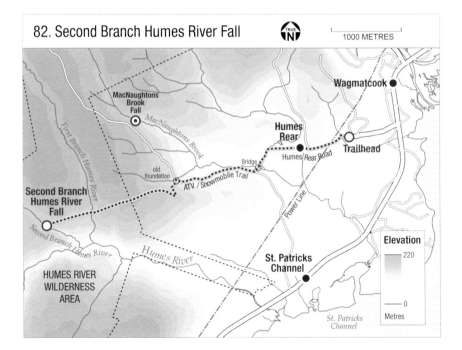

The hike: Humes River Fall has been on my list of places to explore ever since I noticed a hollow spot in the canopy in the middle of the woods. Since the mid-2010s, there has been an effort to develop a trail system to the fall and well beyond. Once the top of the ravine is reached, the roar of the river and waterfall is very noticeable, especially at times of high water. The slope to the base of the fall is moderate, and no rope is required. The base of the fall is quite large and is a perfect spot to relax, eat, and just contemplate this hidden gem. There are also some large cliffs surrounding the waterfall that, with a cleaning, would probably be good for rock climbing.

From where you parked, start walking/biking/snowshoeing on the marked trail. The first 3 km (1.9 mi) of the trail is the continuation of the Humes Rear Road as it becomes narrower and ultimately an ATV and/or snowmobile trail. There is a loss of elevation at first to a large wooden bridge over MacNaughtons Brook. After the first bridge, you cross another smaller brook and then walk uphill to a Y intersection. Turn to the right and hike 1.5 km (0.9 mi) uphill to the narrow, wooded trailhead. There are lots of markers in the trees on the left of the road, and the narrow, woodland trail really begins here. The trail passes by an old rock wall and rock foundations, then it ascends a small hill. The first 1 km (0.6 mi) or so has been cleared of trees to make way for the trail. Following this stretch, the trail is flagged, but no further improvements had been made as of October 2016. The flagged route goes down one small valley (First Branch of the Humes River), goes back uphill, and finally make it to the fall on the Second Branch of the Humes River. There is some undergrowth and thickets of evergreen in some spots to go through, but hopefully future trail construction will make the going easier. Thanks to waterfall enthusiast E. Quigley for letting me know about the new trail!

Bonus fall(s): There is another waterfall on this trail system. It is located on MacNaughtons Brook. It can be accessed via a narrow trail located off the main ATV/snowmobile trail in a location 1 km (0.6 mi) to the northwest of the flagged entry to the narrow trail leading to the Second Branch Humes River Fall.

83. Black Brook (Middle River) Fall

Type: Drop, tiered
Height: 15 m (50 ft)
Best season(s): Spring, summer, and fall
Access: Trail
Source: Black Brook
Distance (one way): 1 km (0.6 mi)
Difficulty: Moderate

Elevation: 120 m/yd
Hiking time: 1 hour
Land ownership: Crown
Maps: 11K02-V3
Nearby waterfall(s): Second Branch
Humes River Fall
Cellphone coverage: Y

Finding the trailhead: From Highway 105 west of Baddeck, turn onto Middle River West Road and then turn left onto Gairloch Mountain Road. After 1.5 km (0.9 mi) and at the Y intersection with Indian Brook Road, turn left onto Gairloch Mountain Road. Within 100 m/yd after the intersection, pass over a small wooden bridge and go uphill to some flagging tape on the left side of the road located 2.1 km (1.3 mi) after crossing the bridge. Park here and follow the flagging tape into the woods in a southerly direction.

Trailhead: 46°11'06.3"N, 60°49'02.9"W   **Waterfall:** 46°7'20.13"N, 60°58'39.16"W

The hike: This is a waterfall that captured my attention a while ago. I was looking at some old maps of this valley and I noticed a caption of a "Fine Fall" on the lower reaches of this brook. I explored this area and walked up the first 1.5 km (0.9 mi) of the valley, but never found a large waterfall. A subsequent visit in October 2015 led to the discovery of an unofficial path to the fall.

From where you parked on the logging road, the trail is marked with orange, blue, and pink flagging tape all the way to the fall. It traverses a mostly maple and beech mature forest that is covered by ferns on the ground. The trail goes down slowly for the first part but then becomes very steep at the end. Someone has put up some ropes but be extra careful before using them. Once you reach the bottom of the valley, the waterfall is only a few more steps upstream.

Bonus fall(s): Continue on Middle River West Road to a bridge 700 m/yd before you reach Maclennans Cross Road. Stop and explore the unique geology and small falls downstream of that bridge.

83. Black Brook (Middle River) Fall

TRUE N

500 METRES

MacKenzie Brook
Indian Brook Road
Indian Brook
Garloch Mountain Road
Middle River West Road
Mill Road
○ **Trailhead**
Black Brook
Macquarrie Road
○ **Black Brook**
(Middle River)
Fall

Elevation
240
0
Metres

84. MacRae Brook Falls

Type: Drop, tiered, fan
Height: 15 m (50 ft)
Best season(s): Spring and fall
Access: Bushwhack and river walking
Source: MacRae Brook
Distance (one way): 3 km (1.9 mi)
Difficulty: Difficult to extreme
Elevation: 250 m/yd

Hiking time: 3 hours
Land ownership: Nature reserve
(pending)
Maps: 11K02-W2
Nearby waterfall(s): Black Brook (Middle
River) Fall
Cellphone coverage: Y

Finding the trailhead: From the Cabot Trail between Hunters Mountain and Lower
Middle River, turn onto Crowdis Mountain Road and follow it for 9 km (5.6 mi).
Turn right onto an unnamed secondary road at 46°11'40.7" N, 60°50'26.7" W. Drive
1.2 km (0.7 mi) and then turn right. Drive 950 m/yd and turn left. Drive all the way to
the end of this logging road and park.

Trailhead: 46°11'06.3" N, 60°49'02.9" W   **Waterfall:** 46°10'46.01" N, 60°48'46.45" W

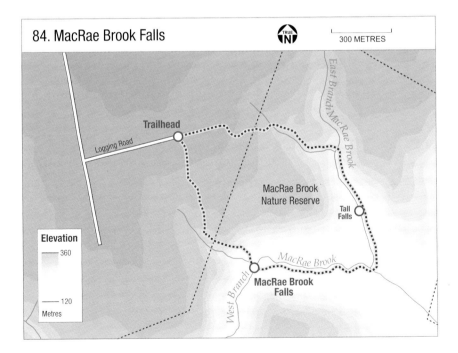

84. MacRae Brook Falls

The hike: A good portion of MacRae Brook is now protected as a nature preserve in the heart of Cape Breton and makes for great hiking terrain. It should be emphasized, though, that this hike is not for the faint-hearted. To explore this ravine requires a good sense of direction and stamina. However, you will be rewarded by the sight of a pristine hardwood valley filled with waterfalls!

From where you parked on a plateau, head east into the Acadian forest to a small brook that has carved a small ravine. The brook has lots of cascade-type falls, but the geology of this particular ravine prevents any tall fall formation. This secondary brook flows eventually into the East Branch of MacRae Brook, and then bigger falls start to appear. There are lots and lots of small ones until you reach the largest fall on the East Branch with a total drop of 21 m (70 ft). A short hike downstream of this fall leads to the confluence with the West Branch MacRae Brook. The forest down there is a treasure. The mature maple, beech, and birch trees are numerous and the canopy is high above your head. Tall ferns unfortunately hide everything, and the bashing of shins on hidden objects is inevitable! After walking 450 m/yd upstream, there is a mini Shangri-La of waterfalls. There are two falls coming down the side walls of the ravine as well as two large falls in the main branch of the brook. The pools at the base of the main falls are very deep and begging to be swum. To exit the ravine and return to the trailhead, climb and follow the side of one of the brooks coming off the sidewall of the ravine heading in a due north direction.

Bonus fall(s): For the explorers, on the north side of Crowdis Mountain Road lies the ravine carved by MacDonald Brook. At least two significant waterfalls are located in this ravine with the largest located at 46°09'47.3" N, 60°52'29.5" W. There are no trails leading to these falls.

85. Egypt Fall

Type: Tiered
Height: 18 m (60 ft)
Best season(s): Spring and fall
Access: Trail
Source: MacFarlanes Brook
Distance (one way): 750 m/yd
Difficulty: Moderate

Elevation: 100 m/yd
Hiking time: 20 minutes
Land ownership: Private and crown
Maps: 11K03-Y2
Nearby waterfall(s): Black Brook (Middle River) Fall, Martha Brook Falls
Cellphone coverage: Y

Finding the trailhead: In Upper Margaree (north of Lake Ainslie), turn onto Egypt Road. Drive 2.2 km (1.4 mi), and then turn right onto Pipers Glen Road. Continue for 1 km (0.6 mi) or until you see flagging tape and a sign on your right. Park here.

Trailhead: 46°11'46.31"N, 61°7'26.86"W   **Waterfall:** 46°11'37.07"N, 61°7'35.76"W

The hike: This waterfall is well known in Nova Scotia and is one of the largest that is accessible via a trail less than 1 km (0.6 mi) long. The name of the fall is confusing as Egypt Brook is actually another brook located close by, and Pipers Glen is the name of the hill feature located above the fall. The trail goes downhill the whole way from the road to the base of the fall, which means you need to keep some energy to get back up! In front of the falls is a large flat area with a small stand of hardwoods where you can relax and have a meal. The fall itself is at least 18 m (60 ft) high and separated into two main tiers, and it is the widest I know of in Nova Scotia. The upper tier has a pool at its base that could be used as a semi-private soaking spot.

From where you parked, follow the path down to the river and fall. The trail is well marked and goes downhill the whole way from the road to the base of the fall. The last 100 m/yd toward the stream is moderately steep. Ropes are in place to help you down.

Bonus fall(s): For the adventurous, there are four known falls on the brook running in parallel to the north of MacFarlanes Brook. Mount Pleasant Brook has two waterfalls on its main branch and two on the same tributary.

85. Egypt Fall

TRUE N

300 METRES

Elevation
280
100
Metres

Egypt Brook

Egypt Road

Pipers Glen

Trailhead

Pipers Glen Road

MacEachins Brook

Egypt Fall

86. Tompkins Brook Fall

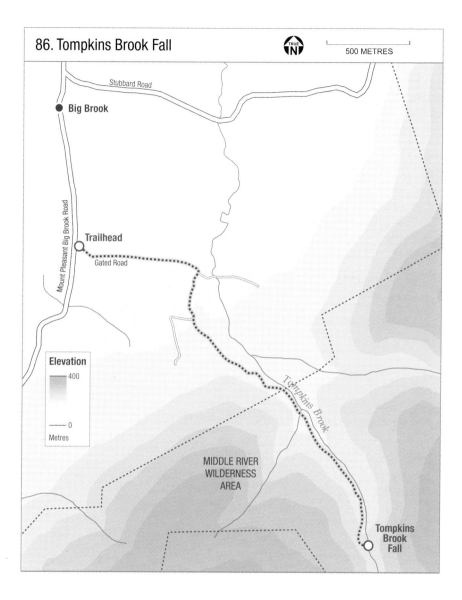

TRUE N

500 METRES

Stubbard Road

Big Brook

Mount Pleasant Big Brook Road

Trailhead

Gated Road

Tompkins Brook

Elevation

400

0

Metres

MIDDLE RIVER
WILDERNESS
AREA

Tompkins
Brook
Fall

86. Tompkins Brook Fall

Type: Drop, slide
Height: 15 m (50 ft)
Best season(s): Spring and fall
Access: Bushwhack and river walking
Source: Tompkins Brook
Distance (one way): 3 km (1.9 mi)
Difficulty: Moderate

Elevation: 200 m/yd
Hiking time: 2 hours
Land ownership: Private
Maps: 11K06-Z5
Nearby waterfall(s): Egypt Fall, Martha Brook Fall
Cellphone coverage: N

Finding the trailhead: Take the Cabot Trail to North East Margaree. Turn onto Mount Pleasant Big Brook Road. Turn left onto an unnamed secondary road approximately 1 km (0.6 mi) past the Stubbard Road. Park here.

Trailhead: 46°16'56.97"N, 61°1'38.89"W   **Waterfall:** 46°16'03.36"N, 61°00'18.59"W

The hike: The thought that I wished I lived in Cape Breton occurred to me when I rounded one last bend of the Tompkins Brook and faced a largely unknown 15 m (50 ft) plus waterfall. During the winter months I often pore over satellite imagery of places I would like to explore in the upcoming year. Near North East Margaree are some deep valleys around the Twelve O'Clock Mountain. I soon spotted a hole in the canopy that might indicate a waterfall. In October 2016 I took the gamble and visited the location. I was not disappointed. The area around Tompkins Brook is absolutely gorgeous with moss-covered rocks and smaller cascades all around. The trees in this valley have grown to gigantic sizes. The fall itself plunges from the plateau higher up into the ravine, creating the space in the canopy. A short climb on the hill on the right-hand side is all that is required to get a birds-eye view of the fall and also to see another 4.5 m (15 ft) fall further upstream.

The hike starts on a gated road off the Mount Pleasant Big Brook Road. A walk of 800 m/yd down this road leads to a secondary road to the right before you cross Tompkins Brook. The secondary road leads to a logged area, and a smaller trail continues on the left side of the clearing. This trail leads close to the brook. There are signs of an old woods road almost all the way to the fall but it has been many decades since it was in use. Once you reach the brook, a hike of approximately 1.5 km (0.9 mi) upstream is necessary to reach the fall. Just before reaching the main fall, there is a multi-tier 6 m (20 ft) fall. The main fall remains tucked away just behind the next bend of the brook.

Bonus fall(s): The Twelve O'Clock Mountain area is a treasure trove of unexplored falls. In the fall of 2017, A. Hooper and I explored a good-size gorge with countless waterfalls on MacRae Brook, which flows into Middle River. The bulk of the waterfalls were located in an area around 46°12′46.9″ N, 60°59′49.9″ W. There are no trails leading to these falls.

87. Bothan Brook Fall

Type: Slide
Height: 15 m (50 ft)
Best season(s): Spring
Access: Bushwhack and river walking
Source: Bothan Brook
Distance (one way): 1.5 km (0.9 mi)
Difficulty: Moderate to difficult

Elevation: 200 m/yd
Hiking time: 1.5 hours
Land ownership: Wilderness area
Maps: 11K07-W5
Nearby waterfall(s): Tompkins Brook Fall, Martha Brook Fall
Cellphone coverage: N

Finding the trailhead: On the Cabot Trail between Hunters Mountain and Middle River, take the Crowdis Mountain Road (which becomes Highland Road) for 16.6 km (10.3 mi) and turn onto a secondary road at 46°15'19.9" N, 60°49'08.3" W. Continue on this road for about 2.5 km (1.5 mi), then turn to the right onto another logging road. Drive another 4 km (2.5 mi), keeping on the main road, and park.

Trailhead: 46°16'38.4" N, 60°52'35.4" W   **Waterfall:** 46°17'0.29" N, 60°52'42.96" W

The hike: Inspired by a description in Fletcher (1877), one fine day in early June 2017, I followed a well-maintained logging road to reach an area within 300 m/yd of the top of the ravine. The descent into the ravine was moderately steep and well-forested. Upon reaching Bothan Brook, a walk downstream leads to a small fall of 6 m (20 ft), which was blocking my path to the gorge. After walking around this fall, I detected an opening in the canopy: a waterfall was ahead! A very delicate descent on the north side of the brook in a very thick evergreen forest led to the area immediately downstream of the 15 m (50 ft) fall. The south side of the brook in this area has some rocky shear walls preventing access to the stream and could be described as gorge-like. The fall is a Cape Breton classic as it plunges first and then careens down the rock wall into a deep pool at its base. A walk further downstream of the main fall leads you past a few more insignificant falls until you arrive at a moderate slope out of the ravine, making this visit a loop hike back to your car.

From where you parked, head due north and down the ravine to the brook. Once you reach the brook, follow your GPS to the fall.

Bonus feature: Southwest of Bothan Brook lie the First to Fourth Gold Brooks, which flow into the Middle River. There are some old gold mine adits to visit off the Second Gold Brook located 4 km (2.5 mi) south of Bothan Brook. The trail to access the adits starts on Gold Brook Road at 46°14'27.1" N, 60°55'07.6" W, off the Cabot Trail to the north of Upper Middle River.

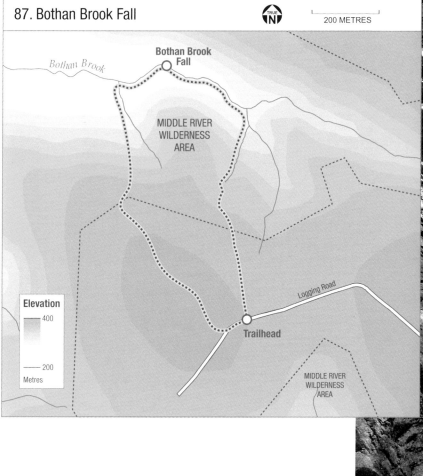

87. Bothan Brook Fall

TRUE N

200 METRES

Bothan Brook

Bothan Brook Fall

MIDDLE RIVER
WILDERNESS
AREA

Logging Road

Trailhead

MIDDLE RIVER
WILDERNESS
AREA

Elevation

400

200
Metres

88. Martha Brook Fall

88. Martha Brook Fall

Type: Drop, slide
Height: 23 m (75 ft)
Best season(s): Spring and fall
Access: Bushwhack
Source: Martha Brook
Distance (one way): 900 m/yd
Difficulty: Extreme (very steep terrain)

Elevation: 120 m/yd
Hiking time: 1 hour
Land ownership: Wilderness area
Maps: 11K07-W3
Nearby waterfall(s): Tompkins Brook Fall
Cellphone coverage: N

Finding the trailhead: In the Margaree Valley, turn onto Fielding Road. The road will ascend 380 m/yd toward Frasers Mountain. Continue for 8.3 km (5.1 mi), then turn left onto a logging road at 46°22'33.6" N, 60°53'05.7" W. Continue straight for 1 km (0.6 mi) and park here. At this point, follow a secondary logging road on the left as it descends toward the ravine created by Martha Brook.

Trailhead: 46°22'06.2" N, 60°52'57.6" W   **Waterfall:** 46°23'2.04" N, 60°53'27.19" W

The hike: An extreme hike down a ravine in the heart of the Highlands of Cape Breton Island leads to a beautiful and hidden 23 m (75 ft) waterfall. The forest on the slope of the ravine is a nice mixture of mature beech and birch trees. The ground is covered by a deep layer of moss. Be careful of the ravine's slope as the terrain beneath the moss is made up of large individual boulders. As such, numerous holes are hidden from sight and you can easily turn your ankle. After making it all the way down, you are rewarded by this beautiful waterfall that cascades down on the pink-coloured rock wall.

From where you parked, take the old logging road heading west and toward Martha Brook. At the end of the old logging road, enter the woods. The bushwhack leads you through a forest composed of small trees that have grown quite close to each other. After only a few minutes, you emerge on the side of an extremely steep-sided ravine. Descend the ravine to reach the falls.

Bonus fall(s): In the Margaree Valley, take the Egypt Road and find the Nile Brook bridge close to Ross Road. Follow this brook upstream for 2 km (1.25 mi). At this point hike further upstream on the tributary on the right (South Nile Brook). Another 1 km (0.6 mi) or so will bring you to a series of waterfalls surrounded by rock walls and steep ravines.

89. Lavis Brook Falls

TRUE N

200 METRES

Lavis Brook Falls

MARGAREE RIVER WILDERNESS AREA

Margaree River

Lavis Brook

Trailhead

5317 Road

Portree

Elevation

300

50

Metres

West Big Intervale Road

Hatchery Road

89. Lavis Brook Falls

Type: Drop, tiered, cascade
Height: 12 m (40 ft)
Best season(s): Spring and fall
Access: Trail and light bushwhack at the end
Source: Lavis Brook
Distance (one way): 1.5 km (0.9 mi)
Difficulty: Easy to moderate

Elevation: 100 m/yd
Hiking time: 1.5 hours
Land ownership: Wilderness area and private
Maps: 11K07-V2
Nearby waterfall(s): Rocky Brook Fall, Turner Brook Fall, Martha Brook Fall
Cellphone coverage: N

Finding the trailhead: In Margaree Centre, drive on West Big Intervale Road to Portree. Approximately 50 m/yd before the bridge over the Northeast Margaree River, turn left onto the road that may have signage as 5317 Road. Drive 15 m/yd and park by the entrance to a house on the right.

Trailhead: 46°24'04.9"N, 60°57'57.2"W   **Waterfall:** 46°24'41.76"N, 60°58'18.62"W

The hike: This is an easy hike to a few delightful falls near Portree in the North East Margaree Valley area. By the side of a house, a road leads to a pasture where the Lavis Brook flows into the Margaree River. Hike in the pasture toward the valley located to the east and look out for signage to the fall. Lavis Brook exits the Highlands plateau in a narrow valley. There are a few 3-6 m (10-20 ft) falls to contemplate before you reach the final and tallest fall on this brook. A charming 12 m (40 ft) waterfall is hugged in on all sides by sheer rock walls in an area surrounded by a mature mixed forest. From where you parked, the trail begins off this shared driveway as it veers to the left and down a slope to the fields beyond. You will see the signage for the hiking trail from this point and also the Lavis Brook Valley in front of you as well as flagging tape in the woods.

Bonus fall(s): To visit some unknown waterfalls on a tributary of Stewart Brook, drive to Kingross and turn left on Kingross Cross Road. Immediately after the bridge over the Northeast Margaree River, turn right on Big Intervale Road and drive 1 km (6 mi) to where Stewart Brook emerges from the hills on your left. Hike 1.1 km (0.7 mi) upstream to the tributary. The falls are located another 200 m/yd upstream on this tributary.

90. Turner Brook Fall

Type: Fan
Height: 30 m (100 ft)
Best season(s): Spring, summer, and fall
Access: Bushwhack and river walking
Source: Turner Brook
Distance (one way): 1 km (0.6 mi)
Difficulty: Extreme

Elevation: 200 m/yd
Hiking time: 2 hours
Land ownership: Wilderness area
Maps: 11K10-V5
Nearby waterfall(s): Rocky Brook Fall
Cellphone coverage: N

Finding the trailhead: From the Cabot Trail in St. Joseph du Moine (near Chéticamp), turn onto Pembroke Lake Road and go up the Highlands. After reaching Pembroke Lake, drive a further 1.6 km (1 mi) and turn left at the major Y intersection. The road will go down a wide valley and back up on the other side. Once at the bottom of this valley, you will cross Forest Glen Brook. The trailhead is located a further 4.5 km (2.8 mi) away from Forest Glen Brook. The worst part of this road is in this

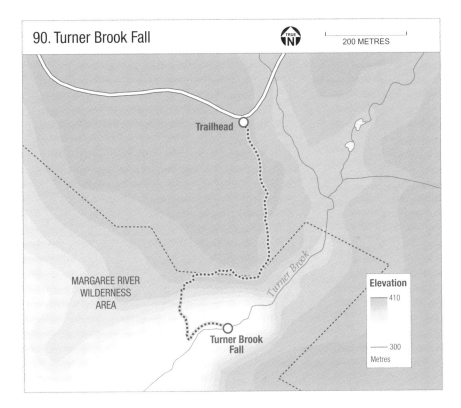

valley, especially when you are going back up to the top of the Highlands. A 4x4 is your only option or your mountain bike. Park near the culvert that contains Turner Brook. Follow the west side of Turner Brook to the fall.

Trailhead: 46°30'35.82"N, 60°55'18.48"W   **Waterfall:** 46°30' 22.34"N, 60°55'20.05"W

The hike: This is another extreme hike to discover a seldom seen 30 m (100 ft) waterfall located on Turner Brook. It should only be attempted by serious and experienced outdoor enthusiasts! The walk to the fall begins higher up on the plateau instead of close to the brook because of the numerous and thick alders. Furthermore, the path to the base of the fall is not close to the top of the waterfall as there are huge cliff walls on either side. Walking on the Highlands plateau is fairly easy as the trees are widely spread apart and the ground is mostly covered by ferns. A hike of approximately 500 m/yd leads to the top of the fall. A short hike west on the same contour line is necessary to reach an open and mature deciduous forest on the gorge slope. The gorge sides are steep, but there are lots of trees to hold onto on the downslope. Once at the brook's edge, there are a few minor falls downstream, but the main attraction lies upstream. Just below the main fall is an area to circumvent as rock walls plunge directly into the brook on either sides. Upon reaching the base of this waterfall, it will be hard to believe that such a unique location exists in this province.

Bonus fall(s): The western branch of Turner Brook also contains very hard to reach waterfalls as it plunges from the top of the Highlands toward the Margaree Valley.

91. Rocky Brook Fall

Type: Drop, tiered, and slide
Height: 46 m (150 ft)
Best season(s): Spring, summer, and fall
Access: Bushwhack and river walking
Source: Rocky Brook
Distance (one way): 1.2 km (0.75 mi)
Difficulty: Extreme

Elevation: 300 m/yd
Hiking time: 4 hours
Land ownership: Wilderness area
Maps: 11K10-W5
Nearby waterfall(s): Turner Brook Fall
Cellphone coverage: N

Finding the trailhead: From the Cabot Trail in St. Joseph du Moine (near Chéticamp), turn onto Pembroke Lake Road (or Grand Étang Road) and go up into the Highlands. After reaching Pembroke Lake, drive a further 1.6 km (1 mi) and turn left at the major Y intersection, located 8.7 km (5.4 mi) after you left the Cabot Trail. The road will go down a wide valley and back up on the other side. The worst part of this road is in this valley, especially when you are going back up to the top of Highlands. A 4x4 is your only option or your mountain bike. Continue for 11.5 km (7.1 mi) past the Y intersection mentioned above and park.

Trailhead: 46°32'9.36"N, 60°53'26.74"W   **Waterfall:** 46°31'51.38"N, 60°53'7.42"W

The hike: This is a hike for the truly adventurous and well-prepared outdoor enthusiast. The terrain is extremely steep and the location is one of the most remote in Nova Scotia. Do not try to follow the stream where it crosses the dirt road. The stream gets tangled up in a very large alder patch that will be very difficult to traverse. Instead just go up on the ridge on the south side of the brook. Hiking 800 m/yd leads you to the edge of the gorge created by Rocky Brook. There are very straight and tall rock walls on either side of the fall, so it is imperative to follow the southerly route by staying high on the plateau before attempting a descent into the gorge. The ground is very slippery and treacherous. There are some small cliff sections throughout the forest to navigate around and enough trees growing on the slope to aid the descent. A large apron of rocks approximately two-thirds of the way down is one of the best vantage points of this massive fall. From where you parked, the brook in front of you crossing the road is Rocky Brook and the fall is located about 1 km (0.6 mi) downstream from your car. The culvert is out over that brook as of August 2016.

Bonus fall(s): Additional walking is not really needed on this epic hike. However, if you do make it all the way down the gorge, travel a further 400 m/yd downstream to another major waterfall that can be seen in satellite imagery.

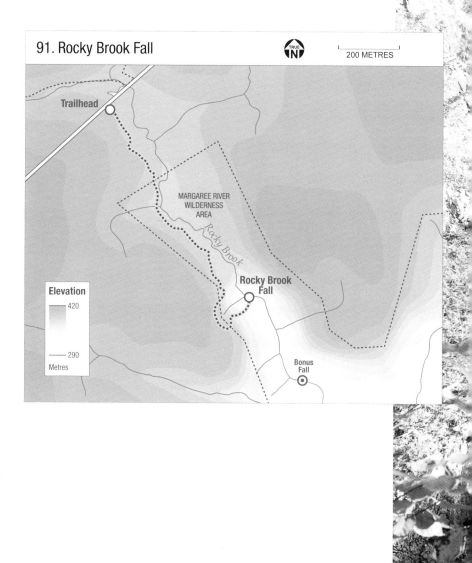

91. Rocky Brook Fall

TRUE N

200 METRES

Trailhead

MARGAREE RIVER
WILDERNESS
AREA

Rocky Brook

Rocky Brook
Fall

Elevation
420
290
Metres

Bonus
Fall

92. Factory Brook Fall

TRUE N

500 METRES

Elevation
350
0
Metres

5309 Road

Grand
Lac

Bonus
Fall 1

Trailhead

CT

Chemin Du Lac

CABOT TRAIL

Power Line

Factory Brook
Fall

ATV Trail

Factory Brook

Bonus
Fall 2

Carding Mill Road

Petit
Lac

Grand
Étang

92. Factory Brook Fall

Type: Drop, tiered, slide
Height: 12 m (40 ft)
Best season(s): Spring
Access: Bushwhack and river walking
Source: Factory Brook
Distance (one way): 2.5 km (1.6 mi)
Difficulty: Moderate

Elevation: 440 m/yd
Hiking time: 1 hour (main fall only)
Land ownership: Private
Maps: 11K11-Z4
Nearby waterfall(s): Farm Brook Fall, Fiset Brook Fall
Cellphone coverage: N

Finding the trailhead: Drive the Cabot Trail between Margaree Harbour and Chéticamp. In Grand Étang, turn onto Chemin du Lac. Turn left at the Y intersection 200 m/yd later. From this point on, follow Chemin du Lac for 1.6 km (1 mi). The condition of the road worsens as you continue, so drive as far as you can and park anywhere out of the way.

Trailhead: 46° 33'17.4" N, W61° 01'15.7" W   **Waterfall:** 46° 33'11.2" N, 61° 00'11.7" W

The hike: Factory Brook near Grand Étang is overlooked and mostly unknown except for the local population. However, Factory Brook has at least three main waterfalls that are worth the detour. The main waterfall is located on the main branch of the brook while two others (bonus falls on map) are located on tributaries of the brook. From where you parked, walk to a small bridge over Factory Brook located at 46°33'27.8" N, 61°00'42.7" W. There is no path to reach the main waterfall, and the first portion of the journey is the most difficult as the forest is quite dense and there are lots of fallen trees. However, after 20 minutes or so you will reach a mature forest and the walking becomes easier. The main waterfall is set into an area where rock walls are prevalent on both sides of the brook. The slope to reach the foot of the main fall is moderately steep. The main fall is located only 800 m/yd upstream of the bridge, but this area sees very little foot traffic, except for moose.

Bonus fall(s): To reach the bonus fall upstream requires an additional 1 km (0.6 mi) of bushwhacking and river walking in the narrowing valley. Upon reaching the bonus upstream fall (bonus fall 2 on map), a very steep climb to the top of the highlands on the slope next to the fall leads to a viewpoint overlooking the whole valley and up to Chéticamp Island in the distance. Following the brow of the mountain, and with a bit of luck, you will intersect an ATV path that will lead you back to the trailhead. One last fall (bonus fall 1 on map) is located just beside the ATV trail in a deep ravine before the long descent to the trailhead.

93. Farm Brook Fall

Elevation
320
0
Metres

Point Cross Pond

CABOT TRAIL

Farm Brook

Power Line

Point Cross

Trailhead

Old Cabot Trail

CT

Farm Brook Fall

500 METRES

93. Farm Brook Fall

Type: Tiered, drop
Height: 23 m (75 ft)
Best season(s): Spring and fall
Access: Trail and river walking
Source: Farm Brook
Distance (one way): 2.5 km (1.6 mi)
Difficulty: Moderate

Elevation: 75 m/yd
Hiking time: 2 hours
Land ownership: Private
Maps: 11K10-V4
Nearby waterfall(s): Fiset Brook Fall
Cellphone coverage: N

Finding the trailhead: At 14115 Cabot Trail, there is a sign for a church (46°34'47.9" N, 61°01'21.9" W). Turn onto the dirt road here and drive up the hill. Park at the back of the church building.

Trailhead: 46°34'47.03" N, 61°1'21.31" W   **Waterfall:** 46°34'13.65" N, 60°59'37.79" W

The hike: This is a nice and surprisingly easy hike to a spectacular fall near Chéticamp. Farm Brook is a typical stream on the west side of the Highlands, which begins its journey high up on a plateau before it carves itself a deep ravine on its way to the Gulf of St. Lawrence.

Near where you parked, the hike starts on a wide and well-maintained ATV/snow-mobile trail. It loses some elevation and then remains on the same contour line as it follows the brook into a V-shaped valley. There are a couple of side trails to the right and left, but keep walking straight. The forest by the brook is quite nice with lots of large deciduous trees. At the end of the road lies a very nice shelter by the side of the river. There is no trail from this point on, but you can tell that people have travelled here before. A short hike of approximately 300 m/yd beyond the shelter leads to a spectacular fall that has a total height of 23 m (75 ft). It's impossible to get the whole fall in one picture as it has numerous drops in a row. A moderate climb of the side ravine slope on the south side of the brook leads to a better view of the top portions of the fall.

Bonus fall(s): An unconfirmed fall is located a further 1.7 km (1.1 mi) upstream of the Farm Brook Fall. This fall shows up on the 1:50 000 topographical maps.

94. Fiset Brook Fall

TRUE N

400 METRES

Cheticamp Back Road

Timmons Drive

Platin Road

Deveau Road

Trailhead

Auvoin Brook

Bonus Fall

Fiset Brook

Elevation

— 300

— 0
Metres

Fiset Brook Fall

94. Fiset Brook Fall

Type: Tiered, drop
Height: 18 m (60 ft)
Best season(s): Spring and fall
Access: River walking
Source: Fiset Brook
Distance (one way): 1.5 km (0.9 mi)
Difficulty: Difficult

Elevation: 80 m/yd
Hiking time: 2 hours
Land ownership: Private
Maps: 11K10-V4
Nearby waterfall(s): Farm Brook Fall
Cellphone coverage: N

Finding the trailhead: From the Cabot Trail, take Chéticamp Back Road. Turn onto Platin Road and follow it for 1.3 km (0.8 mi) until it comes to the side of Fiset Brook. Park here.

Trailhead: 46°36'28.40" N, 60°59'22.55" W   **Waterfall:** 46°35'55.04" N, 60°58'16.35" W

The hike: The headwaters of Fiset Brook are located on the Highlands plateau in the Jim Campbell Barrens Wilderness Area. This is a journey that leads you to a few small waterfalls at first and then a massive fall at the end of a river hike. I guarantee that you will get wet on this hike. There is no path to follow, just the brook itself.

From where you parked, follow the brook upstream through the woods. The river eventually narrows with rock walls on either side. The first fall is easily passable on its south side; the rock wall and scree slope on the north side prevent any passage. After that first fall, the ravine narrows even further, and in some cases you may need to exercise your bouldering skills to keep dry. However, most of the water is waist deep, so there is always the swimming option! The final fall reveals itself after 1.5 km (0.9 mi) of river walking, and it's a beauty. There is a lower fall of about 4.5 m (15 ft) that can be ascended by climbing the rock wall on the north side of the brook. Upstream of the lower fall is a deep pool, and then the main waterfall drops by sheer rock walls on both sides.

Bonus fall(s): Continue on the dirt road to an intersection just ahead. At the intersection go to the left, walk a minute, and follow the first brook you cross to a few very nice waterfalls and some old mill foundations on Aucoin Brook.

95. Faribault Brook Fall

Type: Tiered and drop
Height: 24 m (80 ft)
Best season(s): Spring, summer, and fall
Access: Trail then bushwhacking and
river walking
Source: Faribault Brook
Distance (one way): 10 km (6 mi)
Difficulty: Extreme

Elevation: 800 m/yd
Hiking time: 4-8 hours
Land ownership: Crown
Maps: 11K10-V4
Nearby waterfall(s): Farm Brook Fall,
Fiset Brook Fall
Cellphone coverage: N

Finding the trailhead: On the Cabot Trail heading north past Chéticamp, turn onto
Chéticamp Back Road and drive 2.6 km (1.6 mi) to a dirt road heading west at
46°37'21.0"N, W60°59'10.7"W. Park here. From this point you can hike or, better
yet, mountain bike.

Trailhead: 46°37'21.0"N, 60°59'10.7"W   **Waterfall:** 46°36'09.1"N, 60°54'23.7"W

The hike: This is an extreme journey to a remote and challenging gorge near Cape
Breton Highlands National Park (CBHNP). This is not a hike for just anybody.
Stamina and rock climbing skills are required to safely make it into this gorge,
and out again. The route to the fall requires 10 km (6 mi) one way and an ascent of

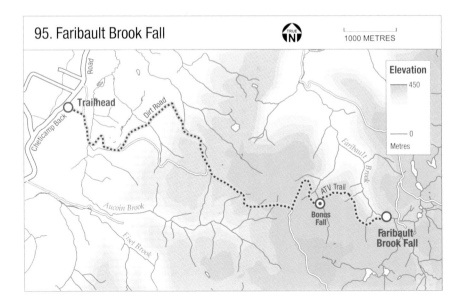

800 m/yd. Faribault Brook is named after one of two geologists who criss-crossed this province in the 1880s and '90s to map out most of Nova Scotia.

The first part of the journey is the ascension of the Highlands Mountains. Toward the top, there is a spectacular view all the way to the Grande Falaise and Presqu'Ile in the CBHNP. The next portion of the hike is on ATV/snowmobile trails that lead toward the Faribault Brook area. The terrain off-trail near the gorge gets surprisingly steep quickly. There are a few cliffs that reach all the way to the trail and standing on them affords a good viewpoint of the Faribault Brook valley down below. The whole descent is only 100 m/yd or so, but the slope percentage can reach up to 70%. Using some bouldering skills it is possible to reach an area right next to the brook. In this area, there are three consecutive 6-9 m (20-30 ft) falls. However, the most impressive sight is downstream as the water plunges one last time through a narrow slit and disappears into the gorge below. The gorge downstream cannot be accessed from upstream as there are sheer walls on both sides of the stream that would be at least 30 m (100 ft) in height

From this point on, the journey upstream will lead you past a few more decent-sized falls of 3-9 m (10-30 ft). The journey finishes at a gorgeous two-tier waterfall. The upper fall is the tallest at about 18 m (60 ft) with a deep pool at its base, and the second fall drains that pool over a fall of approximately 6 m (20 ft). The climb out of this area is also challenging as there are some very steep sections with few trees to hold onto and sharp drops on every side.

From where you parked, follow the road by mountain bike for approximately 10 km (6 mi) until you reach the rim of the gorge at 46°36'07.8" N, 60°54'40.8" W. From here there is no trail to the gorge and falls. The gorge is at 46°36'10.2" N, 60°54'32.1" W and the main falls at 46°36'09.1" N, 60°54'23.7" W. Again, this is a very extreme hike in a remote area of the province and only serious explorers should attempt it.

Bonus feature: A neat feature is located before reaching the gorge and falls—the trail skirts an old, shallow gold mine adit.

96. Goose Cove Brook Falls

Type: Slider, tiered, drop, cascade
Height: 8, 24, 18, 30 m (25, 80, 60, 100 ft)
Best season(s): Spring and fall
Access: Bushwhack and river walking
Source: Goose Cove Brook
Distance (one way): 3.5 km (2.2 mi)
Difficulty: Moderate to difficult

Elevation: 250 m/yd
Hiking time: 3 hours
Land ownership: Private (downstream) and wilderness area
Maps: 11K07-Y5
Nearby waterfall(s): North River Fall, Timber Brook Fall, Great Falls
Cellphone coverage: N

Finding the trailhead: Drive the Cabot Trail toward North River Bridge. Drive 11 km (6.8 mi) from the intersection at the base of Kellys Mountain to Goose Cove. After the bridge over Goose Cove Brook, turn left onto Meadow Road. Continue until you see power lines over the road. Park here

Trailhead: 46°16'4.04" N, 60°38'7.37" W

Waterfall: 46°15'56.1" N, 60°39'31.5" W (Fall 2 on map)

The hike: The waterfalls on Goose Cove Brook have been on my list of places to explore ever since I read an article stating that this brook had the highest number of waterfalls in all of Cape Breton. After visiting most of them, I am inclined to partially agree as surely some other brooks may have as many or more, but just haven't been explored yet.

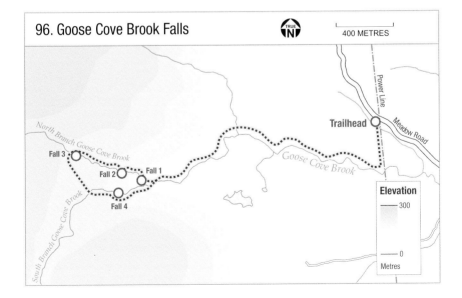

From where you parked, follow the power lines south of the road until you reach the ravine carved by Goose Cove Brook. From this point, follow the brook upstream through a mixed forest for approximately 2.5 km (1.6 mi) until you either stumble upon an old woods road or you reach the confluence of the two main tributaries of the brook at 46°15'52.03" N, 60°39'23.48" W. There is one major fall occurring on the brook before you reach this point as well as an extensive gypsum and karst topography on the hills on either side of the brook just upstream of this first fall. At the confluence of the two brooks, follow the north branch. The north branch has an immediate reward of a 6 m (20 ft) slider fall in front of you. Climbing past this first fall and walking another 200 m/yd leads to a series of falls with the topmost measuring at least 21 m (70 ft). The only way to bypass this fall is to climb the steep valley on the eastern side of the fall. Once you reach the top, a further walk along the tributary leads you past countless other falls of 3-6 m (10-20 ft) in height. A walk of 500 m/yd is well rewarded by the final fall on this branch. This fall of approximately 18 m (60 ft) has a true drop and is surrounded by large rocky cliffs on either side. It is a perfect spot to relax and have lunch. From this point, it is highly recommended that you traverse the plateau in a southeast direction for 300 m/yd to meet the southern tributary. Once you reach the tributary, a short hike downstream of 200 m/yd leads first past two falls with a combined height of 12 m (40 ft) and then to the tallest fall of this system. The tributary at this location loses approximately 30 m (100 ft) in one drop although the water tends to cling to the rock surface all the way down. A view all the way to the highway on Kellys Mountain can be observed from the top of this waterfall.

Bonus fall(s): Continue on Meadow Road for 3 km (1.9 mi) from the power lines until you reach MacLennans Brook. Follow it 1.8 km (1.1 mi) upstream to a 15 m (50 ft) waterfall.

96. Goose Cove Brook Falls

97. North River Fall

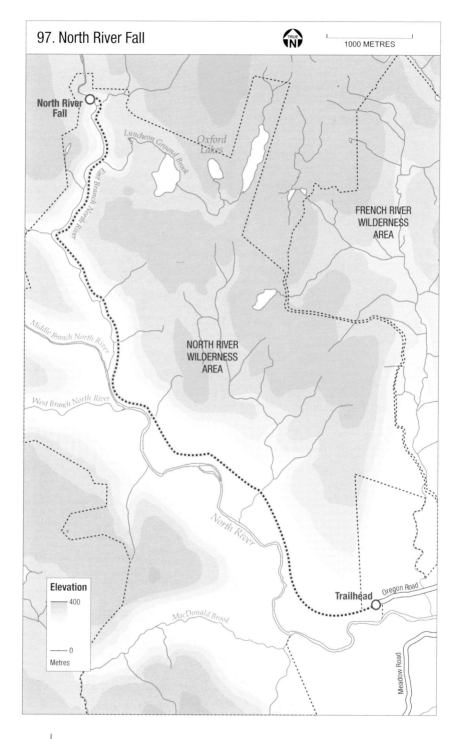

1000 METRES

North River Fall

Luncheon Ground Brook

Oxford Lakes

East Branch North River

FRENCH RIVER WILDERNESS AREA

Middle Branch North River

NORTH RIVER WILDERNESS AREA

West Branch North River

North River

Elevation
— 400

— 0
Metres

Trailhead

Oregon Road

MacDonald Brook

Meadow Road

97. North River Fall

Type: Drop
Height: 30 m (100 ft)
Best season(s): Year-round
Access: Trail
Source: North River
Distance (one way): 9 km (5.6 mi)
Difficulty: Moderate (distance)

Elevation: 680 m/yd
Hiking time: 6-8 hours
Land ownership: Wilderness area
Maps: 11K07-Y3
Nearby waterfall(s): Goose Cove Brook Falls, Timber Brook Fall, Great Falls
Cellphone coverage: N

Finding the trailhead: On the Cabot Trail northeast of Baddeck, drive to North River Bridge. On the east side of the bridge across the North River, turn onto Oregon Road and drive to the end, where you will see the entrance to the North River Fall Provincial Park and the trailhead. Park here. Trail contact info if necessary: Nova Scotia Provincial Parks: (902) 662-3030.

Trailhead: 46°19'05.6" N, 60°39'40.4" W   **Waterfall:** 46°22'13.76" N, 60°41'58.86" W

The hike: North River Fall is located deep in the North River Wilderness Area. The hike to the fall is 9 km (5.6 mi) one way, so plan your schedule accordingly. If you do visit this immense fall, you won't be disappointed. I strongly believe that the North River Fall is probably the tallest fall in Nova Scotia in terms of a single drop.

The trailhead is marked with a sign where you parked. The trail at first is quite broad and is used to access the many pools found in this section of the river. There are some small tributaries to traverse in this section and some foot bridges have been constructed to help. A little distance past the midpoint of the hike, the trail will veer into the East Branch North River, and this is where the trail becomes a little more challenging. The valley narrows quite a lot, and the trail has been constructed in such a way that you need to cross the river a few times. Unfortunately, bridges on this section may be out of commission due to the heavy ice flows in the spring. Unless it's the middle of summer low flow, your best bet is to stay on the east side of the river at all times. That is, unless the bridges are in working order, in which case use them. After a challenging hike of 9 km (5.6 mi), you are rewarded with a huge waterfall of 30 m (100 ft).

Bonus fall(s): In the fall of 2017, I explored a series of three formidable waterfalls on the West Branch North River that were all around 18 m (60 ft) in height with fellow waterfall enthusiast A. Hooper. The West Branch North River exits into the Main Branch North River in an area located midway through the hike to North River Fall. However, these waterfalls are more easily reachable via logging roads off the Highland Road.

97. North River Fall

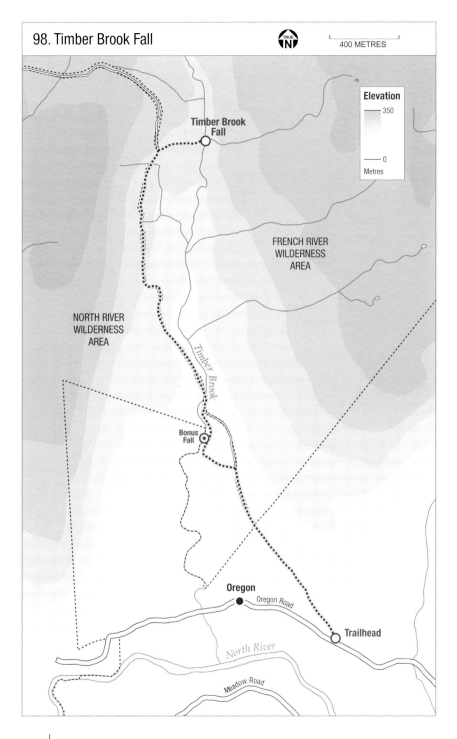

98. Timber Brook Fall

400 METRES

Timber Brook Fall

Elevation
— 350

— 0
Metres

FRENCH RIVER
WILDERNESS
AREA

NORTH RIVER
WILDERNESS
AREA

Timber Brook

Bonus
Fall

Oregon
Oregon Road

Trailhead

North River

Meadow Road

98. Timber Brook Fall

Type: Drop
Height: 18 m (60 ft)
Best season(s): Spring and fall
Access: Trail and bushwhack
Source: Timber Brook
Distance (one way): 4 km (2.5 mi)
Difficulty: Moderate (distance)

Elevation: 300 m/yd
Hiking time: 3 hours
Land ownership: Wilderness area
Maps: 11K07-Y4
Nearby waterfall(s): Goose Cove Brook Falls, Timber Brook Fall, Great Falls
Cellphone coverage: N

Finding the trailhead: On the Cabot Trail northeast of Baddeck, drive to North River Bridge. On the east side of the bridge over the North River, turn onto Oregon Road. Drive for 2 km (1.25 mi) and park.

Trailhead: 46°19'6.92" N, 60°38'28.25" W   **Waterfall:** 46°20'39.46" N, 60°39'0.67" W

The hike: Timber Brook is one of the main tributaries of the lower reaches of the North River and is a worthwhile destination as it contains at least seven main waterfalls. The ATV/snowmobile trail is for the most part well maintained and could easily be used with mountain bikes to decrease the time spent hiking. The forest in this part of Cape Breton is gorgeous with tall mature deciduous trees surrounding it. Do keep in mind that there is no marker at the point where it is necessary to leave the trail to see the fall so a GPS is your best friend on this hike. The main fall on Timber Brook is a breathtaking true drop fall with water cascading off the rock face as it plunges into a deep pool at its base.

From where you parked, there is an ATV or snowmobile trail starting on the right. Walk the trail for about 3.15 km (2 mi). The trail gains elevation and crosses Timber Brook after 1.5 km (0.9 mi). Continue on the trail past the bridge for another 1.5 km (0.9 mi) or so. At this point (46°20'37.9" N, 60°39'13.0" W), your GPS (highly advised) should point to the fall on the right of the trail. Bushwhack 300 m/yd to the base of the fall.

Bonus fall(s): There is a series of six falls located downstream of the bridge on the trail. These falls are not the easiest to explore as the terrain is very steep, but they are well worth the effort.

98. Timber Brook Fall

99. Great Falls

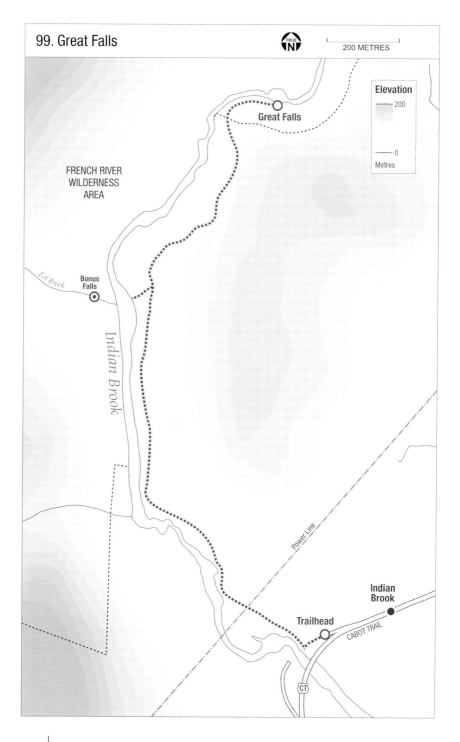

99. Great Falls

Type: Drop
Height: 8 m (25 ft)
Best season(s): Year-round
Access: Trail and bushwhack
Source: Indian Brook
Distance (one way): 2.5 km (1.6 mi)
Difficulty: Difficult to extreme
Elevation: 220 m/yd

Hiking time: 2 hours
Land ownership: Private and wilderness area
Maps: 11K07-Z3
Nearby waterfall(s): Goose Cove Brook Falls, Timber Brook Fall, Pathend Brook Falls
Cellphone coverage: N

Finding the trailhead: On the Cabot Trail, drive about 12.5 km (7.75 mi) north of North River Bridge. Once you arrive on the north side of the bridge over Indian Brook, stop and park.

Trailhead: 46°22'18.25" N, 60°32'1.94" W   **Waterfall:** 46°23'5.58" N, 60°32'10.29" W

The hike: The Great Falls is certainly not tall, but it is surrounded by enormous rocky cliffs on all sides. The height of those cliffs and the large pool at the base of the fall certainly warrants the name of Great Falls. If you wish to see the falls from the base, just before the cliffs appear on both sides of the fall, there is one small area where a down climb from the cliffs on the south side is possible. Bouldering or climbing skills are required to navigate this down climb. Alternatively, and if the river has a low flow, ford the river twice to get to the base of the Great Falls.

From where you parked, the unofficial trail to the fall starts on the north side of the bridge after you pass a driveway to a house. The trail is well marked as it traverses a mixed forest before reaching a power line corridor. It continues on the opposite side of the corridor and follows the edge of some tall cliffs on the side of Indian Brook. After walking 1.3 km (0.8 mi), you reach a mature evergreen forest, and the trail descends a moderate slope all the way to the brook. (The fall you see on the opposite side of the brook is the bonus fall.) From this point on, follow the brook upstream, first on cobble rocks and then bypassing some small cliff sections. Here the brook narrows. At times of high water, cliffs plunge down on the north side of the brook all the way to the water. There are not enough ledges to use to circumvent this feature unless you don't mind wet feet. Ford the brook to the north side, walk upstream, and again ford the stream to the south side to get the best vantage point of the fall.

Bonus fall(s): The 12 m (40 ft) waterfall on Eel Brook can be seen on the way to the Great Falls. Another bonus fall lies nearby in Tarbotvale. Off the Cabot Trail, turn onto West Tarbot Road. Drive 700 m/yd to the bridge over Barachois River. Walk 2.2 km (1.4 mi) upstream from the bridge to a magnificent waterfall with a huge pool at its base. Approximately 500 m/yd before the fall, a small gorge is present on the Barachois River.

99. Great Falls

100. Pathend Brook Falls

CAPE SMOKEY
PROVINCIAL
PARK

Pathend Brook
Falls

Trailhead

Elevation

— 350

— 0
Metres

CT

CABOT TRAIL

Pathend Brook

Gulf of
St Lawrence

500 METRES

100. Pathend Brook Falls

Type: Slide, drop
Height: 6, 6, 15 m (20, 20, 50 ft)
Best season(s): Spring and fall
Access: River walking
Source: Pathend Brook
Distance (one way): 2 km (1.25 mi)
Difficulty: Moderate

Elevation: 130 m/yd
Hiking time: 1.5 hours
Land ownership: Pending wilderness area
Maps: 11K09-V4
Nearby waterfall(s): Great Falls
Cellphone coverage: Y

Finding the trailhead: Take the Cabot Trail to a point about 2.5 km (1.5 mi) south of the entrance to Cape Smokey Provincial Park. At this point, just before the Cabot Trail climbs the very steep Smokey Mountain, there is a sharp 180-degree turn. Park here.

Trailhead: 46°35'0.57" N, 60°23'47.11" W   **Waterfall:** 46°35'21.24" N, 60°24'48.69" W

The hike: The waterfalls at the head of Pathend Brook can be clearly seen from satellite imagery of this area. The images look very promising, with large swath of white where the brook leaves the Highlands plateau and plunges into a high-sided ravine. The first two 6 m (20 ft) falls are on top of each other and are followed by the larger fall. What is unique about this waterfall is that it has carved a box canyon out of solid rock. The fall careens down 15 m (50 ft) on the rock wall before plunging into a deep pool at its base. The rock walls on all sides of the pool prevent a frontal view of the waterfall unless you are willing to swim. Thanks to A. Crowley for sharing a hint to this location with me.

From where you parked, follow the brook upstream. The thin forest is mostly composed of smaller birch and beech trees in the lower elevation with conifers starting to appear at higher elevation. Eventually you reach the long swaths of white, which reveal themselves to be large scree slopes. Persevere a little further to reach the falls. A short climb to the right of the smaller falls leads to the final and massive terminal fall.

Bonus feature: Continue north on the Cabot Trail as it climbs Smokey Mountain. At the top and to the right is the entrance to the Cape Smokey Provincial Park. A 5 km (3.1 mi) one-way trail leads from the parking lot of the park all the way to a view point overlooking South Bay Ingonish and the Middle Head spit in the middle of the harbour.

References

Billard, A. *Waterfalls of Nova Scotia: Thirty-six of Nova Scotia's Most Attractive Waterfall Sites and the Trails That Lead You to Them.* Dartmouth: Sand Dollar Productions, 1997.

Faribault, E.R. *Carleton-Kemptville Gold Area, Yarmouth Co, Nova Scotia.* Geological Survey of Canada Map 1814. Ottawa: Geological Survey of Canada, 1920.

Fletcher, H. *Report on Exploration and Surveys in Cape Breton.* Geological Survey of Canada Map 1875-1876. Ottawa: Geological Survey of Canada, 1877.

Fletcher, H., and E.R. Faribault. *Report on Geological Surveys and Explorations in the Counties of Guysborough, Antigonish, Pictou, Colchester, and Halifax, Nova Scotia, from 1882 to 1886.* Ottawa: Geological Survey of Canada, 1887.

O'Reilly, G.A. "From the Mineral Inventory Files. Are the Bridgeville Iron Mines and New Lairg Copper Mine Siblings?" *Nova Scotia Minerals Update* 20, no 1 (Winter 2003): 3. https://www.novascotia.ca/natr/meb/data/pubs/ftmif/mif21n1.pdf.

Robert, J.A., C.F. Armstrong, and O.E. Prud'homme. *Preliminary Geological Map of the Torbrook Iron District, Annapolis Co.* Annual Report–Geological Survey of Canada. Vol. 16. Ottawa: Geological Survey of Canada, 1905.

Index

Benoit Lalonde has lived in Nova Scotia since 1999. He has published 15 peer-reviewed studies on the ecology of the Atlantic region, and is a top contributor to www.trailpeak.com. He currently works as an ecological risk evaluator for Environment and Climate Change Canada and is an avid hiker, mountain biker, climber, telemark skier, spelunker, explorer, and kayaker.